Tips and Tidbits
A Book for Family Day Care Providers

Janet Gonzalez-Mena

National Association for the Education of Young Children
1509 16th Street, N.W.
Washington, DC 20036–1426

**National Association for the Education of
 Young Children**
1509 16th Street, NW
Washington, DC 20036–1426
Website: http://www.naeyc.org/naeyc

The National Association for the Education of
Young Children (NAEYC) attempts through its
publications program to provide a forum for
discussion of major issues and ideas in our field.
We hope to provoke thought and promote professional growth. NAEYC wishes to thank the
author for donating her time to the development
of this book as a contribution to our profession.

Library of Congress Catalog Number: 91–067248
ISBN Catalog Number: 0–935989–47–1

NAEYC #303

About the cover: The quilt reproduction is "Getting
into the Purple," by Wendy Holland, Sydney,
Australia, 1984, 82 x 97½ inches, collection of the
quiltmaker. First published in *The Quilt Digest*
#4; used by permission of The Quilt Digest Press.

Photo credits: pages 1, 13, 19, 22, 29, and 59/
Subjects & Predicates; page 6/Hildegard Adler;
pages 9 and 41/© 1991 Marilyn Nolt; page 16/
Trinity Photos; pages 25, 47, and 49/Nancy P.
Alexander; page 35/© 1991 Michaelyn Straub;
page 39/Scott Belland; page 43/Rich Rosenkoetter;
page 57/Ellen Galinsky.

Book design and production: Jack Zibulsky with
Polly Greenberg

Copyediting and proofreading: Penny Atkins and
Betty Nylund Barr

Editorial assistance: Julie Andrews

Printed in the United States of America.

Table of Contents

Introduction   v

Part I. Effective Ways To Change Unacceptable Behavior   1

1. Discipline: Some considerations   2
2. Alternatives to punishment   3
3. Modeling as discipline   4
4. Allowing children to experience the consequences of their acts   4
5. Praise as a motivator   5
6. Changing the behavior of infants   6
7. Discipline and the environment   7

Part II. Dealing With Individual Children   9

8. Coping with the strong-willed child   10
9. The toddler with the twin issues of power and control   11
10. Victims   12
11. The child who tattles   13
12. Lying   14
13. Potty mouth   15
14. Caring for the difficult child   17

Part III. Helping Children Cope With Feelings   19

15. Expressing feelings   20
16. Fears   21
17. Anger   22
18. Squabbling: When should adults intervene?   23
19. Helping children deal with separation   24
20. Channeling exuberance   26
21. Encouraging hesitant children to take risks   27

Part IV. Teaching and Learning About How To Get Along in the World   29

22. Infant education   30
23. Toddler and preschool education   31
24. Expanding sex roles in the family day care home   32
25. Teaching prosocial skills   33
26. Teaching self-help skills   34
27. Nurturing curiosity in children   36
28. Risk taking   37

Part V. Caregiving Routines 39

29. Infant caregiving routines   40
30. Preschool caregiving routines   41
31. Two views of naptime   42
32. Preventing eating problems   44
33. Toilet training   45
34. Cleaning up   46

Part VI. Play 49

35. Providing for free play   50
36. Setting up the environment for play   51
37. The benefits of outdoor play   52
38. Taming the troops: Ideas for calming
         groups of children   53
39. Using play activities to teach cooperation   54
40. The benefits of pretend play   55

Part VII. Parents 57

41. The importance of parents   58
42. Parent-provider relations   59
43. Some specifics about communicating
         with parents   60
44. Multicultural issues   62

Conclusion 64

Additional Resources 65

Information About NAEYC 66

Introduction

This isn't the complete book of family day care with all the information you need about how to open and run a family day care home. This is, as the title says, "Tips and Tidbits," bits and pieces of practical information and advice designed to help you in a concrete way solve some of the problems you confront in your day-to-day work with children.

This book assumes that you are working in the field and have some experience but are not yet a veteran. Most long-time providers already know all this, I suspect. They may find what I've written here validating. Also, they may find they don't agree with everything, but perhaps even the items they disagree with may give them something to think about.

Although these tips and tidbits are based on sound theory, the theory doesn't show much. I urge you, however, to go beyond my little hunks of advice and explore what's behind them. Start by clarifying for yourself what you believe. We all have our own theories about children's behavior. I challenge you to pull out your theories and take a look at them. Where you don't have a theory to explain something, create one!

As you read this book compare how your beliefs and theories fit with the ones behind these tips and tidbits. Find out more about theory. This is not a short-term project. It will take some reading and talking. I have listed some resources for each section in the back of the section. Classes help explain theory. It's tough to just read on your own, but plenty of providers have educated themselves in just that way.

The point of exploring theories is not just to sound smart but to give some thought as to how theories translate into actions. As you well know, what counts when you work with children is how you behave—and how they behave. Theory alone is useless; but theory combined with thoughtful action is very powerful. It's the way we all get better at what we do.

Because the most common age group in family day care is preschoolers, this book focuses on children between infancy and school age. Some sections, however, apply specifically to toddlers, and some specifically to infants. Some information pertains to all age groups. Most of the information on the preschoolers also applies to school-age children. I have also tried to take into account that most family day care providers serve mixed-age groups.

In the Caregiving Routines section, I have acknowledged that philosophy and practices may vary. In that section I gave more than one point of view. This same theme is also evident in the Parents section. Please generalize this attitude to the other sections as well, although I did not specifically mention variation very often in the rest of the book. I do want you to know that I don't believe there is just one right way to do anything when it comes to child care and education.

Although not a provider myself, I have worked closely with family day care throughout various periods of my career in early childhood education. In the mid-1970s I directed the Neighborhood Child Care Program in San Mateo County, California, run by the Family Service Agency. I not only supervised a group of family day care providers who were employees of the agency, but I provided resources, support, and training for them. More recently (1990-1991) I was involved in writing and implementing a grant for training family day care providers at Napa Valley College, the community college where I teach in the Early Childhood Program. Also, since 1986 I have been writing a column for family day care providers in a newsletter published by Community Resources for Children, a local child care resource and referral agency. So, although I do not work with children in my own home, I have plenty of contact with people who do. Also, I raised five children of my own, so I have some idea of what it's like to have a crowd of children of various ages around.

I've been told my tips and tidbits meet a need. I hope you will find them useful.

Effective Ways To Change Unacceptable Behavior

1

Discipline: Some Considerations

What Works. The first consideration is "what works." Have you ever watched a child trying to get a puzzle piece to fit? When the child has tried the same approach over and over and is just ready to yell at the puzzle piece, it's likely that you'll suggest, "Try something else." The same message goes for discipline. If you try an approach several times and it doesn't work, **try something else.**

Side Effects. The second consideration is side effects. Is your approach to changing behavior at the expense of *self-esteem?* Children who pick up the message that they are bad will act that way; those children who think they are stupid will have a hard time learning. Punishment and criticism are likely to produce side effects. It is better to find effective ways of changing behavior that leave self-esteem intact.

Inner Controls. The third consideration is inner controls (*self*-discipline). With a toddler or some new children, you expect to always have to be on top of things. You know you must constantly enforce limits or provide control; but eventually you'll expect the children to respect the limits and to control themselves—most of the time, at least. They will be more able to do this if you give them reasons for your limits. ("If you pull the cat's tail, she might bite you." "If you jump on the couch, you'll wear it out, and then we won't have a nice couch to sit on.")

If you agree that the point of discipline is to move from outer controls to inner controls, you will not only give reasons, but you'll change

"I don't want to catch you hitting him." (Implied message: ". . . but if you can get away with it, it's okay.")

to

"I won't let you hit him." (Implied message: "I'll provide the control for you now. Eventually I'll expect you to provide your own self-control.")

In spite of the number of experts who try to lead you to believe that their method of discipline is the best one, you know very well that no one way works all the time for all children. There is no "right way" to discipline. You know lots of right ways. You know, too, that the best discipline is discipline that *works,* that *enhances self-esteem,* and that *leads to self-control.*

2
Alternatives To Punishment

Punishment is not the most effective way to discipline. Punishment creates side effects such as fear, anger, and loss of self-confidence. These feelings get in the way of the lesson the punishment is trying to teach. Here are some other, more effective ways to change undesirable behavior:

Stop the behavior. Provide control for the child. If a simple "no" and a quick explanation work, fine; if not, provide physical control. Sometimes a simple touch will do it. Other times you need firm physical control, even to the point of removing the child from the situation.

Prevent the behavior from happening. Prevention is even more effective than prohibiting. Family day care providers get very good at predicting what is going to happen. When a squabble escalates, a firm "I won't let you hit your sister" while holding the child's hand gives both children the security of knowing that you are in control of the situation.

Teach desired behavior through modeling. If you are trying to teach a child to be gentle to your dog, you must do it in a nonaggressive way. Aggressive or rough behaviors are the very ones you are trying to eliminate. You need to show him how to gently pet your dog. Touching the child gently at the same time gives a stronger message. Take every opportunity to model the behavior you are trying to teach. Modeling is a powerful tool.

Ignore behavior that is designed to attract your attention. (But, of course, don't ever let one child hurt another.) Most tantrums fit into the category of attention grabbers. So does toilet talk and squabbling. Instead of using up your energy reacting to the "button pushing" that children learn early on, develop your observation skills so you can note the times your children are being good. Pay lots of attention to them when they are doing what you want them to do, and they will have less need to "push your buttons."

Allow children to experience the consequences of their acts (within reason). The child who leaves the table during lunch can be told that the time to eat is when lunch is served. If he chooses to leave, then he will have to wait until afternoon snack to eat again.

Any of these methods can be *punishing* if done in a way that hurts the child. The key to avoiding punitive overtones is to remain calm, firm, respectful, and confident that changing the behavior is best for the child, you, and the other children.

3
Modeling as Discipline

The word *discipline* comes from the same root word as the word *disciple*, which means "one who follows a master." If you think of yourself as the master—the example setter—you'll be more effective in your use of discipline.

What you are is more powerful than what you do, which is more powerful than what you say. I believe in this paraphrase of the old saying, but we're often guided by the other old saying, "Do as I say, not as I do." Aren't we all guilty, at least occasionally, of telling children to do what we don't do and to be what we aren't?

Take, for example, messiness. If you tend to be a tidy person, you model that tidiness, so you can expect children to follow your directions as well as your example. If your tendency is to leave *your* things all around, you may have problems getting children to pick up their things.

Here's another example. Some adults yell at children to be quiet (I've done it myself). However, it's more effective to lower your voice when talking to a screaming child or a group of noisy children.

What about aggression? Adults usually respond to aggression in children with even more aggression. Of course, family day care providers don't hit children, but I know I'm often tempted to handle an aggressive child rather roughly because I feel angry about his or her behavior. My suggestion is, to try hard to respond to aggression with calm firmness and then model gentleness. It works!

This approach to discipline by modeling is not the "natural way"; it takes some getting used to. Many of us were raised with models of the "Do-as-I-say, not-as-I-do" school of thought. It is not easy to change our own behaviors—much easier to focus on those of the children. Yet if we are to continue growing in our ability to discipline children, paying attention to modeling is an important consideration.

4
Allowing Children To Experience the Consequences of Their Acts

Jason is ruffling the hair of the old, trustworthy cat. "She doesn't like it when you do that," he is told. He continues to do it.

"This is the way to do it." He is shown how to pet the cat.

He continues to stroke the cat in the wrong direction. The cat gets up and walks away.

Feedback is a powerful learning tool.

Here are some other examples. Amber pours her milk carefully into her glass, then sets the glass down on the edge of her fork. The glass tips and the milk spills. "Watch the glass" warns the provider, but she's too late. Instead of scolding, she hands Amber a sponge. Amber mops up the spill, pours more milk, then watches carefully how she sets her glass down.

Mikey is playing when called over to listen to a story. He has already heard several announcements that story time is approaching.

He says, "No!"

The provider is calm, but clear that this is when the story will be read, not later. After story time is naptime. "It's your decision," she says.

He sits stubbornly watching the other children gather around the provider. The minute the story is over, he asks for a story. When gently told "No," he begins to fuss and whine.

"I'm sorry you're ready now and you weren't before, but it's naptime now." The provider is kind but firm. Mikey cries himself to sleep.

It's hard to watch a child experience frustration or disappointment when you have the power to prevent it, but we all learn from such experiences. Rather than rescuing these children or going back on her word, the provider allowed each to experience the consequences of his or her act or decision.

Some guidelines ensure that the experience is a positive learning experience:

1. Don't allow a child to come to harm. Jason's provider knew the cat wouldn't scratch.

2. Predict, don't threaten. The point is to allow children to learn, not to punish them.

3. Be understanding about the child's disappointment or frustration.

5
Praise as a Motivator

Praise is like pollen. Sprinkle some around and praised behaviors multiply.

I watched a group of preschoolers at breakfast. "More toast!" demanded one.

"Please may I have more juice?" asked another.

"Good asking!" said the adult to the second child, ignoring the first.

Immediately the first child said, "Please may I have more toast?" even though she was neither corrected nor criticized for demanding rather than asking.

Praise works. Being noticed is rewarding. Some children are only noticed when they are causing problems. These children need to be "caught being good." That's not easy when their undesirable behavior is very noticeable and their desirable behavior is practically nonexistent. It's not easy when you are used to more criticism than praise yourself. It's not easy, but it's worth the effort.

Here are three tips to make praise an effective motivator:

1. Use praise generously, but don't "gush."

2. Be honest. Children tend to disregard fake praise just as they do gushing praise.

3. Be specific. Give feedback about actions rather than issuing global judgments. "Good asking!" instead of "Good girl!"

Remember that the goal of motivating children is to get them to internalize the motivation. You don't want them to always be dependent on your feedback. Eventually they should behave in desirable ways because they want to, because they find satisfaction in doing so.

To help the process along, teach children to praise themselves. "You must feel very good about how hard you worked on cleaning that table" tunes children in on their own inner rewards. Personal satisfaction is the best motivator of all!

6
Changing the Behavior of Infants

Infants need their own special section when discussing changing behavior. Discipline, which is the subject of this section, doesn't apply to babies in the same way that it applies to toddlers, preschoolers, and school-age children.

What kinds of behaviors do infants show that need changing, and how do you change them? Difficult infant behaviors—behaviors that bother adults—fall into two categories: communication of needs and expressions of feelings. The focus of the adult response should be on meeting the needs and accepting the expression of feelings rather

than changing the behavior. When the adult reads the messages correctly and responds, while accepting the feelings, the behavior changes on its own.

Behavior is communication—at all stages—but during infancy it is particularly vital that behavior be regarded as communication rather than as something to change. For example, a one-month-old is screaming her lungs out. Your objective, of course, is to soothe her; but if you respond to her need rather than just use soothing techniques, you'll be more effective. You will also teach her that communication brings a responsive adult— not one who just lulls and distracts but one who understands. That's a valuable lesson not only on the value of communication but on the power this child has to bring attention to her own needs. She begins to build trust and self-esteem as well as communication skills. Of course, the trick is to figure out the need of a one-month-old, who can't tell you anything except by screaming. Is it food? Often that's the case, but not always (even though food can be a soother and mask the real need). Is it discomfort? Will a burp or change of position help? Maybe she needs the security of being held, or wrapped tightly, or maybe she needs the freedom of being able to move around. Maybe she is tired and needs to sleep. The person who can best tell you is the child herself. Observe, try things out, and observe some more. What is this child telling you she needs?

Some infants are harder to understand than others. They cry, and you don't know what they need. Some have a much lower discomfort threshold, some have high activity levels, and some fuss and cry more than others. You won't always be a successful interpreter. It isn't easy to meet needs or accept feelings, but the payoff is worth it in the long run as these same fussy babies grow into trusting children who can put into words how they feel and what they need.

7
Discipline and the Environment

An interested, involved child is less likely to need discipline than a bored, restless one. What is in the environment and how you set it up has a lot to do with how much guidance and control the children in it need.

Good planning and adequate supplies and materials make all the difference in the world. The environment carries a message about how to behave in it. Your play environment should call out to the child, "Get involved, play, be creative, explore, experiment." Your resting environment should say, "Quiet now, relax, settle down." Your eating environment should say, "Eat!" and should make it easy for children to focus on food and to help themselves to the extent they can.

Age is an important consideration in setting up an environment. What you need for infants is different from what you need for toddlers, preschoolers, and school-age children. If you have a mixture of ages, you need to figure out how to create spaces that are developmentally appropriate for each—not that they must necessarily be separate spaces. The family room of many homes provides an example of how the same space can serve varying ages.

When designing for specific age groups, you should think about scale. Infants need furniture, equipment, and space appropriate to their small size, just as older children need larger furniture, more challenging equipment, and larger play spaces. With some thought, you can design a learning/care environment that is the proper scale for each of its inhabitants.

Mobility is another consideration. All the children in your care need freedom to move around. For infants, of course, this need demands little space. Even toddlers can find lots of ways to use their bodies in a relatively small space. When children reach school age, they need areas for running and vigorous ball playing. The park or school yard may have to become a periodic, temporary extension of your day care home.

Acoustics can make a difference. If sound isn't muted, the normal, joyful (and not-so-joyful) noises of a group of children become a source of overstimulation, which can result in behavior problems. Sound muting often occurs naturally in family day care because homes usually have stuffed furniture and carpeting. Of course, if you have the children in a room that has more hard than soft surfaces, you'll find that sound is amplified.

The activities you present can also make a difference. If you have a variety of age-appropriate activities for the children to choose from—some that are open ended (such as crayons, paint, playdough, or sand) and some that are closed (such as puzzles and games)—most children will find something to do. The occupied child is far less likely to get into trouble than the unoccupied child—although, of course, just keeping them busy isn't your major goal in presenting activities—enhancing development is.

Children are also influenced by order or disorder in the environment; to what extent is an individual matter, but it is worth considering. A bit of chaos is good for all of us, but we each have our level of tolerance—also of neatness. Find the right point on the scale for you and for your group of children.

For Further Reading

Greenberg, P. (1991). *Character development: Encouraging self-esteem & self-discipline in infants, toddlers, & two-year-olds* (pp. 167-178). Washington, DC: NAEYC.

Honig, A. S. (1989). *Love and learn: Discipline for young children* [Brochure]. Washington, DC: NAEYC.

National Association for the Education of Young Children (Producer). (1986). *Discipline* [Film], with Jimmy Hymes. Washington, DC: NAEYC.

National Association for the Education of Young Children (Producer). (1987). *Discipline: Appropriate guidance of young children* [Film]. Washington, DC: NAEYC.

National Association for the Education of Young Childreen (1986). *Helping children learn self-control: A guide to discipline* [Brochure]. Washington, DC: NAEYC

Stone, J. G. (1978). *A guide to discipline*. Washington, DC: NAEYC.

II
Dealing With Individual Children

8
Coping With the Strong-Willed Child

Being strong-willed is a good character trait. Some of the greatest achievements to humankind have come from strong-willed people; however, being around an obstinate person—one who opposes your every wish or command—can be a big headache. I'm not talking about typical toddler behavior that will pass (discussed next); I'm talking about truly stubborn people—those who have this trait as a prominent and permanent part of their personalities.

Here are some suggestions about how to handle a strong-willed child who continually shows stubborn behavior:

1. Avoid all unnecessary demands. Don't ask the child to do something that you're not prepared to carry through on. If you wish she would do something, but you don't absolutely require it, give her a choice, and then accept it if she doesn't make the choice you wish. Children with choices are less likely to be stubborn. And if they perceive the choice is a real one, they might even choose what you want. For example, "I'd really like you to be here to hear this story, and I hope you'll choose to stay; but if you want to leave you may sit quietly over there and look at a book."

2. Try not to issue challenges. Often you can make a demand as a positive statement rather than an order. "Bottoms belong on chairs" rather than "Get down off the table."

3. When you do make a demand that you know is for the children's best interests, be very clear about what you expect, and be prepared to insist. "You may not hit. I will stop you if you try again."

4. Once you've enforced a demand, don't let protests bother you. Let the child express her displeasure. You can acknowledge the feelings with something like "I know you're unhappy about this ..."

5. Don't allow the child to manipulate you with protests. If you give in or even pay a lot of attention to her refusal to do something, you are teaching her that the way to get you to focus on her is to make a fuss. Give attention when she is *not* fussing.

6. Don't try to rule by fear. Gentle, persistent firmness works better. Threatened children often become even more obstinate.

It helps to recognize that stubborn behavior is normal. Obstinacy occurs naturally when children are thwarted, yet they must learn to accept other people's ways and wishes as well as to control their own. This won't happen overnight—some people have a hard time ever learning this lesson.

A certain amount of stubbornness will serve a person well once she learns to combine it with affection and reason. It's easier to raise a child who goes along with what you want, but is this really your goal? After all, effective childrearing and education should teach children to question now and then, to use their own heads, to make their own decisions, and to take a stand on things they believe in. The problem when this occurs in the early years is that they don't always know what is best for them, and they aren't able to sort out the important issues from the minor ones. Once they learn both of these lessons, stubbornness can be a valuable trait.

9
The Toddler With the Twin Issues of Power and Control

Most toddlers go through a period when they are difficult to get along with. Jason is no exception.

"I'm constantly fighting with Jason," complains Barbara. "I just can't get him to do anything. Every little thing I tell him to do is a big struggle. Sometimes he just comes up to me, gives me a push, and tells me 'No!' when I haven't even said anything to him."

What can Barbara do?

First of all, she can understand that Jason is coming to see himself as a separate individual, one who needs power and control over his actions and his life. Of course he doesn't have the wisdom or skill to really take control or use his power, but someday he will, and Barbara needs to understand that he is practicing for this time to come.

Right now she can find positive ways to approach him when he needs to be told what to do. For example, she can tell him what he is capable of doing instead of what he is not allowed to do. She can say, "You can pat the dog gently," instead of "Don't hit the dog." Instead of "Get down, please," she can say "You can put your feet right here" indicating the floor. This will only work if she is matter-of-fact and confident in her tone of voice. At the slightest hint of bossiness, Jason will take her words as a challenge and do the opposite.

At times it is important to be clear about what is not allowed. "I won't let you throw the blocks" tells Jason that, when necessary, Barbara will use her control to augment his. Then Barbara can give Jason some positive alternatives. "You can throw the paper airplane or the foam ball."

Barbara knows to avoid questions that allow for negative answers. She never asks Jason, "Do you want me to comb your hair?" unless she is prepared to tolerate an unkempt child. She asks instead, "Do you want me to comb your hair now or after snack?" When it is time to take medicine, she asks, "Do you want to hold the spoon yourself, or should I hold it for you?"

Feeling powerful is important for development. Children need to sense that they can make things happen in the world—that they have some control. For the toddler these are especially big issues because they are working on developing independence. At the same time they need restrictions because their abilities to get into trouble are greater than their self-control. Keeping out of power struggles by avoiding challenges and by offering alternatives is a way to grant them their power and still provide the control they need.

10
Victims

Do you have a child who is always getting hit, is constantly picked on, or is a victim? Victims don't just happen; they are created.

Some children learn the "victim role" very early, even in infancy. They can get stuck in this role, continually being picked on by other children, so the victimization continues throughout childhood. It may even become a lifetime pattern.

How do children learn the victim role? They may discover that being a victim brings them attention. Some adults fuss a good deal over a child who gets hurt. They usually do this because they feel sorry for the child or perhaps to remove the attention (reward) from the child who did the

hurting; but this approach backfires because the attention rewards the victim.

Other children don't learn the role by being rewarded with attention but get stuck in it because they just happen to be the object of an aggressor's attack. If their response stimulates the aggressor and they don't know how to keep this from happening again, they may well end up in repeat performances.

What can you do to help children who are continually victimized? Here are some ideas:

1. Don't blame victims. Although they may unconsciously attract attention in one way or another, it is not their fault. They in no way "deserve what they get."

2. Don't teach the victim role by rewarding it. Be calm and supportive or comforting to the receiver of an aggressive attack, but don't lavish your attention on him or her.

3. Prevent aggression before it happens. (That way you remove the reward from the aggressor as well as the victim.)

4. Teach children to avoid attacks. (Most learn this by themselves if they aren't blinded by the victim role.) Some places are safer than others. In the face of danger, it's wise to stick near an adult.

5. Teach children to stand up for themselves by giving clear messages. "I don't like you to hit me!" said emphatically can have quite an impact on an aggressor who is used to children cowering and screaming. Or "I won't play with you if you hit me!" may also carry some weight. If children are too young to make these kinds of statements on their own, say the words for them.

6. Support children who stand up for themselves. Back them up and prevent the aggression from happening.

11
The Child Who Tattles

We all know a child who comes running to tell on somebody every few minutes. "He hit me!" "He's going to dig in your flower bed!" "She colored on my picture!" Tattling is irritating. Why do children tattle?

Sometimes children tattle to get attention. If that is the case, the way to stop it is to withdraw your attention. Don't respond every time a child comes to you with a complaint or story. Do give attention, however, at other times—those times when the child is not tattling. You need to replace the attention the child is used to getting by tattling.

Another reason children tattle is that they don't know how to solve problems. Sometimes adults even invite tattling by being the chief problem solver. "Tell me when you have a problem," they say. Then they spend a good deal of time and energy solving problems for the children. That takes away valuable learning for the chil-

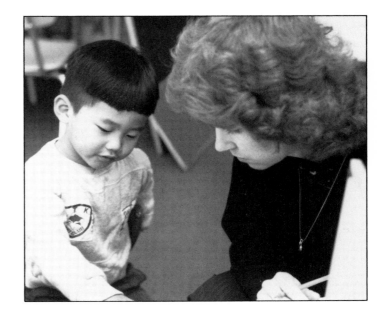

dren involved in the problem and entangles the adult even when he or she need not be.

Instead of providing solutions yourself, help the children do their own problem solving. Start by taking the "tattling child" to the child in question and get them to talk to each other. Stay with them until they talk it out and/or resolve the problem. Help them be honest with each other. Help them express feelings without put-downs.

Many times children in conflict with each other don't need you at all. They can argue it out themselves. Of course, if one is likely to hurt another, you need to be on the spot to prevent this. Or perhaps one is a better arguer than the other; you can use this opportunity to teach the other one assertiveness skills. Those are the times during which you need to be on the sidelines of the conflict. Many times you do not.

If you do need to be present when two children are having a conflict, don't step in as referee. Say what you see is going on, but tell the children what to do as little as possible. This way they'll learn to solve conflicts or at least manage them. If you do all the work for them, they don't learn anything except to come to you the next time they need help.

Here's an example of sports announcing. Amy tells you, "Zach colored on my picture."

You say, "Tell Zach you don't like that."

Amy says, "Zach don't! I don't like it."

You remain silent.

Zach says, "I want you to play with me."

Amy says, "Well, you don't have to color on my picture."

You say, "Zach wanted to play with you, but instead of asking, he colored on your picture." You are talking to the thin air—Amy and Zach have run off to swing together.

If Jake is digging in your flower garden, and a child reports it, that's a different story. That's not a conflict between children; that's a problem between you and Jake. You need to get to Jake and give feedback, quote limits, redirect the energy, and point out consequences.

If the child who is telling on Jake says only, "He's *going to* . . ." it's likely that Jake is just creating a scene rather than actually digging where he's not supposed to. Some children love to send another off to tattle. Jake probably needs your attention as much as the child who tattled does. Give both the attention they need—just don't give it to them when threatening and tattling is involved!

───── 12 ─────
Lying

Many children can't separate what is real from what is not. The younger the child, the more likely this is the case. The early childhood education profession does not use the word *lie* when discussing children under about age three. Young children simply can't distinguish what's real and what's not. They engage in wishful thinking, for one thing, and are sometimes convinced that if they say something is true, it is. They are still sorting out what is fantasy and what is real (and we play along with their view of fantasy-as-real-life with the tooth fairy, Santa Claus, Smokey the Bear, etc.). So if we say Santa flies all over the world in one night, why do we get mad when they say that a bear got mud on the floor?

Sometimes a lie is really a difference in perception. When two children are arguing, each may firmly believe his or her own version of the story. It doesn't help for an adult to step in and decide which is the truth and which is a lie. It is more useful for the adult to help the children sort it out themselves, give each other feedback, and explain their own perceptions. This is excellent practice for problem solving and conflict resolution in adulthood. Let children start it young. Don't decide for them what happened and who was right and who was wrong.

Sometimes children resort to denying the truth because they see it as the only way out, even when directly confronted with the facts of a situation. They obviously believe the consequences of the situation are pretty drastic and feel threatened rather than supported in seeking solutions to the problem. For example, if you ask "Who spilled the milk?" when you know exactly who did it, you're asking for a lie. If you say instead, "I see you spilled the milk. Here is a sponge to wipe it up," you're handing over responsibility rather than inviting the child to try to find a way out.

The best way to deal with lying is to prevent it. Here are two tips for keeping you from having to deal with a child who believes he or she has to tell you something different from what you believe.

1. Don't encourage children to lie by backing them into a corner when you know they've done wrong or made a mistake. If you know a child is guilty, don't ask, "Who did this?" Start from the position that you know what happened. Don't put the child in the position of trying to save face or escape a consequence by going off into fantasy land. It's too tempting for most children, and the younger ones may not even know they are doing it!

2. Be truthful yourself. Honesty is best taught through modeling. If you say there's no more dessert when the refrigerator's full of it, you're teaching lying. If you're willing to engage in fantasies such as fairies and Santa Claus as explanations of how things happen, expect the children to do the same. I don't mean that you can't be imaginative, but do help children sort out what is real from what is not!

13
Potty Mouth

"Poopoo Head!" shouts the two-and-a-half-year-old playfully to see what happens, relishing the sound coming out of his mouth.

"Potty Mouth!" his four-year-old brother shouts back.

Why do young children shout such things at each other? Words are interesting. Words are powerful. Just as young children explore the objects in their environment, so do they explore the words that come their way.

They soon discover what we know—that words can hurt, heal, soothe, calm, or excite.

No wonder when little children discover the power of words, they want to use them. They like getting a strong response. They tend to repeat things that make them feel powerful—like forbidden words. Four-year-olds, in particular, depend on the fact that "swear words," "dirty words," and "bathroom talk" will get a rise out of adults.

Children also use forbidden words because they don't know any better. They hear these words and imitate what they hear. They acquire these words the way they acquire the rest of their vocabulary.

So what can you do about "cleaning up" a child's mouth? Forget the old-fashioned soap mouthwash. There are far better ways that don't harm or degrade the child. Here are some suggestions:

1. Ignore. If the behavior is designed to get your attention, ignoring the behavior will make it go away. There's no reward in yelling "shit" at someone who turns and walks away.

2. Tell the child you don't like the particular word or phrase, and ask her not to say it. (This direct feedback only works if the child *cares* whether you like it or not and is willing to stop using the language.)

3. If the behavior continues anyway, set some limits so it's somewhat under your control. Give the child some words to use that you *do* approve of. Another approach is to assign a special place where swearing is allowed. "Go to the bathroom for bathroom talk" is a rule in some family day care homes.

Whatever you do, stay out of power struggles. As in toilet training, there's no way you can control what comes out of children. Find ways to grant their power and keep yours!

14
Caring for the Difficult Child

A family day care provider assistant—a beginner—in one of my classes wrote to me in a journal, "A young girl in my home is very difficult. She's often violent—she even bites. But today she was in such a good mood—it was like she was a different child. I don't know what was different about today, but I sure did learn something. I know now that no child is really 'rotten.' *There's a beautiful child inside somewhere that needs to be found."*

Every "difficult child" in care or preschool deserves a teacher or day care provider who has learned that lesson early on. What a difference it would make in their lives!

It's a matter of image. When you see a child as difficult, rotten, hard to handle, or aggressive, and you have no other view of him or her, you convey a certain message to that child. The child then reflects the image that you have, in turn reinforcing that same image in your eyes. It's a vicious circle which, once started, may never be broken—even after a lifetime of trying.

But if you are convinced, as my student now is, that *there's a beautiful child inside every child,* you put energy into finding that child. You look hard for signs of that hidden person, and each time you touch her, you add to a new image forming in the child's mind. It's surprising, the power that images have! Our actions are governed by the images we carry of ourselves and of others.

Here are some tips about how to touch this hidden inner child:

• Convey love and acceptance. When a child feels accepted unconditionally, energy for violent, unloving acts can be turned into positive behavior.

• Be concerned about meeting needs. Which of this child's needs are not being met? How far can you go in meeting them while he or she is in your care? Go out of your way to meet every need you possibly can.

• Catch the child being good, smart, kind, or gentle. Pay attention to this behavior when it occurs. Set up situations when it is likely to occur. Avoid situations that trigger the other behaviors.

• Avoid labels. Labels solidify images and make them "real" and permanent. Never use a negative adjective to refer to a child. Label behavior if you must, but even then, label it using specific descriptive terms rather than judgmental ones. ("The child pushes and hits" rather than "The child is mean.")

• Look inside yourself to see what feelings, reactions, and self-images this child triggers. By being honest with yourself, you may shed new light on the situation.

For Further Reading

Derman-Sparks, L., & the A. B. C. Task Force. (1989). *Anti-bias curriculum: Tools for empowering young children.* Washington, DC: NAEYC.

Greenberg, P. (1991). *Character development: Encouraging self-esteem & self-discipline in infants, toddlers, & two-year-olds* (pp. 58-62). Washington, DC: NAEYC.

Jervis, K. (Ed.). (1984). *Separation.* (J. Berlfein, photog.). Washington, DC: NAEYC.

National Association for the Education of Young Children (Producer). (1986). *Culture and education of young children* [Film], with Carol Phillips. Washington, DC: NAEYC.

Riley, S. S. (1984). *How to generate values in young children: Integrity, honesty, individuality, self-confidence, and wisdom.* Washington, DC: NAEYC.

Saracho, O. N., & Spodek, B. (1983). *Understanding the multicultural experience in early childhood education.* Washington, DC: NAEYC.

Savitovsky, D., Baker, K. R., Berlfein, J. R., & Almy, M. (1986). *Listen to the children.* Washington, DC: NAEYC.

Warren, R. M. (1977). *Caring: Supporting children's growth.* Washington, DC: NAEYC.

III
Helping Children Cope With Feelings

15

Expressing Feelings

Children have plenty of feelings. It's their job to express them. The provider's job is to recognize, accept, and validate these feelings. They also need to help children discover ways to calm themselves.

Infants' expression of feelings is different from that of older children because infants have no words. Much of infants' early crying and fussing has to do with communicating needs. It's hard to separate feelings from needs because along with the needs may come expressions of frustration, anger, impatience, even fear. After needs are met come smiles and gurgles of satisfaction and pleasure.

When adults put into words what they see an infant expressing, the baby grows up not only knowing that feelings are accepted, but having also acquired a vocabulary of emotion words. For example, the adult can say, "I know you are hungry. I see how impatient you are with my being so slow!" or "You don't like it when I take that toy away from you, but I'm afraid you'll get hurt. I know it makes you mad when I take it."

If you are a person who was raised in a home that discounted feelings, you may be tempted to say on occasion to a frustrated four-year-old, "Oh, that's nothing to get mad about." When you make statements like that, however, you are denying the existence of something very real to the child.

Children who grow up with adults who deny their feelings, learn to deny feelings themselves. They learn not to feel them. But unfelt feelings don't go away; instead, they just go underground where they influence behavior without the person being aware that this is happening.

Providers must not only accept children's feelings (and also those of the older children in their care) but also accept their own feelings and make decisions about expressing them. It is appropriate to say to a child "I'm really angry right now," but be careful about saying "You made me angry," because that statement takes the ownership of the feeling away from the adult and puts the responsibility for the feeling on the child. We each need to claim our own feelings. We may feel anger in response to something someone else has done; however, that person doesn't make us angry—we are the source of our own anger. It's a subtle distinction but an important one.

How do children learn to soothe themselves when they need soothing? Most discover ways early in infancy, such as sucking a thumb or a fist, petting a blanket binding, or twisting hair. Infants are born with varying abilities to calm themselves. Some can settle themselves early on, and others take weeks, sometimes months, to learn that they have within them the skills to settle themselves down and make themselves feel better. Because this is such an important lesson, adults should see their role as facilitating the learning rather than taking sole responsibility. I won't tell you not to use a pacifier, especially if you or the parent firmly believes in them. I am going to tell you that the more a child can take over the job of soothing himself, finding his own ways of calming down, the better. The pacifier is under adult control with young babies. Adults decide when it can be used; they put it back in the child's mouth when it falls out. The baby has little say in the matter. If the baby gets used to providing her *own* pacifier (like a fist) that is always available, she's in a much more powerful position. She learns that she has the ability to self-calm. That's the kind of learning that lasts a lifetime. Some infant ways change; for example, hair twisting and thumb sucking may become hair *stroking* in the four-year-old. Think about the way you handle your own upset feelings. Do you have a variety of ways to make yourself feel better? Some of them you probably learned as a baby.

16
Fears

The world is a scary place for young children. Things that don't bother adults may terrify children—clowns, sirens, thunderstorms, getting sucked down the bathtub drain, and nameless-faceless creatures, and monsters.

Here are some suggestions for helping young children cope with fear:

1. Take fears seriously. Don't make light of them. What may seem safe enough to you may be terrifying to a young child. Learn to be reassuring without discounting the feeling.

2. Help children to be in control and to make decisions while you offer support and protection. For example, stay nearby while encouraging them to let a friendly dog approach them. Tell them they can choose to pat the dog or just talk to it. When necessary, provide the control they lack. Sometimes your calm presence alone is enough to help them regain control when they lose it.

3. Recognize that fear may not always look like fear. Much fear is disguised as anger. Work sensitively to uncover and understand the real feelings rather than just dealing with the surface behavior. And be aware of when you are showing anger when what you are feeling is fear. Children learn ways of expressing feelings from adults. Be sure you are clear in your expression.

4. Be aware of the power of modeling. Children learn fears from adults. If you show your fear of, say, harmless spiders or snakes, children may easily pick up the same fears. On the other hand, if you show reasonable fear, for example, of a dangerous experience such as approaching an unfenced cliff, your children will come to understand how fear can work to keep people safe.

5. Recognize the value of play in coping with fear. Children very often "play out their fears." Water play in a dishpan can be a means of coping with bathtub fears for example. Allowing children to explore, discover, and experience in safe ways is a good approach to helping them cope with fears.

My best advice for helping children cope with fears is to use your own experience as a guide. We all know what it feels like to be afraid. We all have experienced fear as a protection device. We all having coping mechanisms to deal with the fears that we can't do anything about. By being sensitive as well as supportive, you can help the children in your care learn to use and manage their fears the way you do.

17
Anger

Sometimes angry feelings carry good, clean, strong energy. Children can learn to use that energy to express themselves and work toward problem-solving solutions that eliminate the source of the anger but don't tear down or intentionally hurt other people.

Anger gives extra strength or insight so that a problem that can't be handled well without the anger becomes solvable with the angry energy. Although solutions may be slow in coming, when an angry episode is over, it's over. It's as if a breath of clean, fresh air has washed over the person—like a rainstorm has just passed.

This kind of anger I call honest anger. People who feel, express, and/or act on honest anger are using anger in the way anger was designed to be used. They manage their anger by using various processes to solve the problem and eliminate the reason for the anger.

Sometimes children, instead of using angry energy, learn to hide their feelings. They may even go so far as to hide their anger from themselves. This can happen when children are told *"You shouldn't be angry."*

Sometimes children hide their anger because they are afraid of such strong feelings. They may fear losing control (Don't we all?), Or they may

22

have an image to uphold—perhaps a good girl image or a mature boy image.

Another obstacle to using angry energy is fear of being wrong. In a conflict situation, if you use angry energy to push for your side—your way of doing it—your point of view, you then have to deal with the consequences if the other person was right and you weren't.

Children who aren't encouraged to express and use honest anger learn to manage their feelings in misguided or dishonest ways.

Some children pout and stew. It's as if they have a big pot inside them with just enough fire under that pot to keep it simmering. Then, just as a real stew takes a variety of plain, raw foods and blends them into a glorious whole, so does their stewing process take an incident, add it to the other incidents already in the pot, and, with a blending of spices, create a much bigger mess than the original incident warranted.

Children may pout openly, or they may make themselves very scarce, pouting in private. When asked, they may deny that they're angry, or they may whine and blame others without taking responsibility for their own feelings.

Of course, the best way to teach honest expression of anger is to model it. If you express yourself appropriately, openly, and honestly, children may pick up the ability. If you use anger to solve problems, rather than to accuse, blame, or hurt people, children too will learn to express and use their anger in constructive ways.

18

Squabbling: When Should Adults Intervene?

Squabbling is a fact of life among children who know each other well enough to have differences and feel secure enough to express them. No matter what techniques we use to get rid of squabbling, it will continue to exist as long as children are in care together.

Accepting squabbling as a fact is a necessity for family day care providers. Knowing when to intervene is also a necessity. Here are some guidelines:

1. Don't intervene when a fight is only a play fight and is fun for every one. Some squabbles are pleasurable to the squabblers. Children may argue, even wrestle, and tussle the way puppies do. These play fights need no adult intervention as long as no one is in danger of getting hurt and the adult is not driven to distraction by the activity and noise.

2. Don't intervene when children can settle something themselves without hurting each other. Some squabbles are short-lived if ignored by adults. For example, children, especially toddlers, may feel strongly about possessing something, but once in their possession, the object is quickly abandoned. These kinds of struggles are not worth your attention.

3. Intervene immediately when a child is in danger of getting hurt. Help the children talk it through, providing the matter-of-fact, firm control they may need. Allow them to express their feelings even if the emotions are strong. Don't get caught up in the children's feelings. Remain detached, calm, and slightly apart from the situation when you intervene.

4. Prevent psychological damage as well as physical damage. Stop children from hurting each other verbally, and give them words to express their feelings that relate to actual *behaviors*. For example, help them to say, "I'm mad because you took my toy," instead of "You're mean and ugly and selfish, you brat!" Model this nonabusive way of expressing feelings yourself by stating the feeling and relating it to the behavior rather than by labeling and name calling.

5. Ignore squabbling that is solely an attention-getting device. Sometimes it is enough to just turn your back and walk away. You can tell if the squabble is for your benefit if it stops when you ignore it. If the children seem to be squabbling in order to get your attention, find ways of giving each squabbler more attention each day.

Children learn valuable lessons through squabbling. When they fight, bicker, and argue, they experience an intense relationship. This relationship can help develop social competence. From the simple beginnings of struggling over a toy or a lap, children can learn such important social skills as negotiation, compromise, and give-and-take. They don't learn these skills by always being left alone to work out their problems. They don't learn them if the adult takes care of all the problems, either. They need practice on their own, but with the help of an adult who is willing to stand by to protect and support the learning that is going on.

19

Helping Children Deal With Separation

It's hard to be left someplace new with someone you don't know if you are a young child. Perhaps you can remember those feelings of being small and helpless and away from home. Try to understand what the child who stands sobbing as her mother drives away is feeling.

Here are some ideas about how to help that child cope:

1. Accept the feelings. The child may be scared, lonely, angry, or a combination of all three. Let him know that these are normal feelings and that you understand. Put your understanding into words. Say something like "Your mom had to go to work, and you're unhappy about being left." Don't try to make the feelings go away by simply distracting the child.

2. Handle the situation with the appropriate degree of seriousness. Don't make light of the situation. Don't downplay the importance of the relationship of the child to parent and the degree of suffering the child may be experiencing.

3. Reassure the child that she is in good hands and that the parent will return. Provide a balance of kindly concern and matter-of-fact confidence. Convey the attitude that even though it hurts, the child will survive.

4. Reassure, but don't be *overly* reassuring. If you make too big a deal out of the parent's return, the child may become suspicious. He may begin to wonder why you are making a big fuss if you're really so sure the parent is coming back.

5. Offer support and help with coping. Physical closeness may help, but don't force yourself on a child. Some children do better with an adult close by; others move from the parent to a toy or interesting material put out to be enticing. Sometimes children will play out their feelings with a toy.

6. Welcome things from home. Some children find comfort in a familiar object that they link to home. For some, a familiar pillow, blanket, or stuffed animal may help. The object doesn't have to be a security object—one toddler felt great comfort in the fact that his mother left her purse by his diaper bag (an empty purse).

7. Allow children individual ways of feeling comforted. Some children refuse to remove a sweater, hat, or other piece of clothing. Perhaps they believe the stay is only temporary as long as they don't take off the sweater.

Separations may be difficult on everybody, but they also provide excellent learning opportunities. You're an important part of children's education as you help them develop coping skills. These skills learned in the early years serve the individuals for the rest of their lives.

20

Channeling Exuberance

Young children are power packs of energy. Energy, to be effective, must be channeled along positive lines; otherwise, it produces negative behavior. Here are some tips for keeping the energy of the children who are in your care flowing in positive directions.

1. Give plenty of opportunities for physical outlets and challenges. A simple device such as a truck inner tube in your yard for bouncing on may help. Space to run also helps—if you don't have enough, a local park may be the answer. Children who work their physical energy out of their systems are more ready to settle down and concentrate on quiet activities when the time comes. They also rest and eat better.

2. Allow, even encourage, plenty of sensory, "touchy" experiences. Water play is an all-time winner with children. It's easy on hot days when you can put the children outside with a hose. On other days, you can give them small amounts of water in dishpans or kitty litter trays (unused by kitties, of course). Put the pan or tray on a thick bathmat to absorb the drips. Younger children don't need lots of water; an inch or two will do. Older children may need more, but instead of water, they can find satisfaction with a thin paste of cornstarch and water. It looks messy but cleans up easily once it dries into a fine powder. Sand, of course, is an old standby for "touching experiences."

3. Provide for emotional outlets using such media as art, music, dancing, and dress-up. Emotional energy needs release just as physical energy does. For children to express their feelings through different media, they need materials, props, and above all, *freedom*. An art project with directions to follow and an adult model to copy won't do much for pent-up feelings; paint, a brush, and several pieces of large paper may.

4. Provide for curiosity. Young children have a lot of energy behind their drive to find out all about the world and how it works. Let them explore, experiment, and discover by giving them a safe, interesting, rich environment. Let them look for snails in the bushes, let them try rolling the ball down the slide, let them see what happens when they mix water with sand.

5. Redirect energy that is behind undesirable behavior. If the baby is throwing the toys in the wastebasket, give him a beanbag and a box and show him how he can do the same activity in an acceptable way. If a six-year-old is climbing on your car in the driveway, redirect her to a safe place to climb where she won't hurt anything.

Redirection is a valuable technique. After all, it isn't the energy you want to eliminate—it's the negative behavior. Often you can turn that behavior right around so the same energy is being used in positive ways. The better you get at that channeling, the easier life will be for everyone!

21

Encouraging Hesitant Children To Take Risks

"Don't you want to play?" asks Brook's mother, who ushers her daughter over to where three children are on the floor stacking blocks into a tower. Brook backs away, holding tightly to her mother's hand and looking from her mother's face to that of the provider.

Brook does want to play, but she is aware of the risk involved. If she asks to play, she might be told "No!" Rejection hurts. If she just starts playing, she might still be shoved out or told to leave. Even if she is allowed to play, she takes a risk of stacking the blocks "incorrectly." Being criticized also hurts. Although it may be hard for her mother to understand the risks involved in this situation, Brook is fully aware of them.

When an adult perceives that a child is taking a psychological risk, the adult may wish to protect that child. Risk always involves the possibility of failure, and we all hate to see children fail. It would be safer to just give Brook a few blocks of her own in another part of the room rather than encourage her to approach the other children. Risk, however, also offers the possibility of success. Think about how good Brook feels when she gets up her courage and finds that her approach brings welcome in response.

We can't always protect children from failure, and indeed we shouldn't. Failure can provide important learnings. Of course, continual failure is harmful to self-esteem; therefore, it is important that adults help children be successful as well as let them occasionally fail. Brook can be helped to enter the play situation by

• letting her play by herself close by until she feels brave enough to approach, until she is invited, or until she is naturally incorporated into the activity (this frequently happens);

• suggesting the children include her and perhaps hinting at a role she could take ("Brook could gather all the long blocks for you");

• suggesting that the children include her and then reminding the children how it feels to be excluded if they choose not to include her.

Adults who appreciate risk taking notice when it occurs and praise the child for it. They also appreciate the fearful feelings that may go with risk taking and avoid distracting children from them. Instead they let the children know that they are understood and the feelings are accepted. In addition they offer a sense of support to take courageous action or at least to cope with the situation.

Risk taking is important to growth and learning. Learning often involves challenge, and challenge usually involves risk.

For Further Reading

Greenberg, P. (1991). *Character development: Encouraging self-esteem & self-discipline in infants, toddlers, & two-year-olds* (pp. 75-100, 151-160). Washington, DC: NAEYC.

McCracken, J. B. (1986). *Reducing stress in young children's lives.* Washington, DC: NAEYC.

McCracken, J.B. (1990). *So many goodbyes: Ways to ease the transition between home and groups for young children* [Brochure]. Washington, DC: NAEYC.

IV
Teaching and Learning About How To Get Along in the World

22

Infant Education

Whether you realize it or not, infant care is infant education. Everything you do is educational for infants as they come to learn about the world and the people in it. Caregiving routines are educational, so is free play time. During both of these components of your day care day, infants learn about themselves as they develop relationships with the people and objects around them. You don't need to create activities, develop learning objectives, or engage in infant exercise in order to carry out an educational program in your home. All you have to do is facilitate problem solving. Problem-solving opportunities occur naturally throughout the day as infants cope with, for example, hunger or discomfort, manipulation of objects, separation, or interacting with peers. Through problem solving, babies learn how to make things happen in their world. They gain skills, a sense of self, and a sense of power. What better goals for education?

Looking at infant education from a problem-solving perspective gives clear direction to the adult role. In this approach adults become facilitators rather than teachers or trainers.

Part of the adult's job in providing for infant education is to control the stress level of the baby. Some stress is an important part of learning; too much stress causes the baby to lose focus on solving problems; too little stress leaves the baby without problems to solve.

Another aspect of the provider's role in infant education is to provide attention. Attention is powerful. Babies wither and die without the proper attention. For each individual, there is an optimum amount of attention—and optimum is what you should aim for (not maximum). If attention is lacking, the baby finds ways to get it. You want to make sure that the babies in your care learn to get the attention they need in healthy ways or they may resort to such destructive devices as biting or hitting (not that all babies who bite or hit are seeking attention, but many are).

An old standby rule about adult attention is "Catch kids being good." In other words, if enough attention is given for acceptable behavior, young children won't have such a need to exhibit unacceptable behavior. I'm not, however, telling you to ignore crying. Crying is communication. Babies need attention when they cry. I'm also not advocating heavy doses of praise. We all know how manipulative that feels. I am suggesting that each child in your care—infant or not—should get the attention he or she needs. This isn't an easy task.

Providing feedback is also a part of the adult role in infant education. Children need to know the effect their actions have on the world and on others. For example, when the milk spills, the caregiver can verbalize what happened, without blame or accusations. He or she can then offer a solution by handing the child a sponge and suggesting that the child wipe up the milk. Another example: Little Maria is patting the face of the provider. She puts more energy into the movement, and the pat becomes a slap. "Ouch, that hurt!" exclaims the provider, without a smile.

Modeling is also important to infant education because the children in your care pick up behaviors and attitudes from you. Of course, you can't always be a perfect person, but even your human weaknesses and the way you deal with them are educational for the infants and other children in your care.

23
Toddler and Preschool Education

Infants aren't the only ones who benefit from the adults in their lives taking a problem-solving approach to their education. Just as with infants, developing problem-solving skills is a valuable part of toddlers' and preschoolers' early experience and contributes not only to mental development but to overall development.

On any given day in a family day care home, some children may be working on solving small problems such as how to get a puzzle piece to fit, and others will be concerned with big problems such as how to cope with feelings. Jennifer, for example, may be working on her fear of her provider's large dog, while Josh is coping with the question of whether his mother will ever come back again.

Problem solving crosses all areas of development as children gain competence physically, intellectually, socially, and emotionally. Michael works at carefully balancing one block on top of another in order to build a tower (physical and intellectual problem solving). Jessica is trying to figure out how to get the truck that she wants very much, but that Sue is playing with (social and emotional problem solving).

Family day care providers can help children develop skills as they encounter problems, both big and little, during the course of each day in child care. Here are some hints about how to encourage skill building:

1. Be aware of when problem solving is occurring. The key to this awareness is observation. Watch children as they play, eat, and relate to each other and to you. If you have a problem-solving focus, you'll appreciate the variety of problems children work on each day.

2. Allow children to work on their problems themselves. Don't always be rescuing them. It's tempting to help the child with the puzzle piece, make the block balance on the tower, put the dog outside, or insist that the other child give up the toy; but then you solve the problem for the child, preventing the opportunity for learning and the satisfaction that comes from conquering an obstacle.

3. Help children to be successful. Experienced providers can tell each child's frustration threshold. They know when a child is just about to give up on a problem. They can step in right before this point with a small hint or a bit of help that will keep the child working on the problem. ("I wonder how you could turn that puzzle piece around so it fits better.")

4. Allow failure sometimes. Failure is often good feedback. When the block falls, the child learns that he must balance it more carefully or select a smaller block. The child who has plenty of chances for success can use the lesson he learns from failing. You know which children can experience failure and learn from it, and which ones need every chance for success they can get.

Through the activities and materials you make available, you present a variety of problems for the children. "How can I get the water to stay in this funnel with the hole in the bottom?" "I can glue this collage when it's flat, but how do I make the leaves stick when the collage paper is hanging on the fence?" "If vinegar and baking soda create such a reaction, will sand and water do the same?"

Good problem solvers see themselves as "do-ers"—capable people. They don't run away from problems, and they don't give up easily. The world needs more of this kind of people. No one is in a better position to promote competent problem solving in children than you, the family day care

provider, the person who is with them daily as they play and learn!

24
Expanding Sex Roles in the Family Day Care Home

The early years are when narrow sex roles have the greatest effect on the child's self-concept. What happens in day care can influence children's views about what they can do and how, according to their sex. Their ideas about what they can do when they grow up may be limited. Boys who have never had a chance to nurture may see themselves as incapable of becoming nurses, day care workers, or teachers. Girls who never run or climb may lack physical skills as well as the inclination to become firefighters or police officers.

Did you know that even in this more enlightened age, people still tend to remark to girls about their looks and clothes ("Don't you look pretty today") and to boys about their deeds ("I saw how well you did that"). They tend to help girls more than boys and reward clinging behavior. If adult behavior doesn't change, children's stereotypical views of themselves as boys or girls won't change either.

If you believe in equality of opportunity for both sexes, you might be interested in some ideas of ways to free your home from stereotypes. These ideas follow:

1. Be aware of how you might be treating boys differently from girls. Do you ask for a "big, strong boy" to help you? Ask for a "big, strong child" instead. Notice strength and ability in girls as well as in boys. Also, be sure you notice boys being gentle, nurturing, and caring.

2. Watch the media messages to which you expose children. Find books that show strong, successful women as well as gentle, nurturing men in a variety of occupational roles. If your children watch television, avoid programs that stereotype sex roles.

3. Encourage both sexes to play with all your toys. Girls need to build things, explore, and experiment. Boys need to have access to dolls and dress-up clothes (that should be both male and female).

4. Encourage parents to send children in nonrestrictive clothes. Girls in dresses, ruffles, and slippery shoes can be greatly hampered in their play.

5. Model expanded sex roles yourself. If children don't see adults cross over the invisible boundaries that those adults were raised with about women's jobs and men's jobs, they will incorporate these same boundaries into themselves. This happens even with adults who are trying to teach something different. Modeling is a powerful influence.

25
Teaching Prosocial Skills

All providers set limits for behavior. Limits are an important aspect of discipline, but they aren't the whole story. Children need to know what *not* to do, but they also need to know what *to do*. They need to learn prosocial skills such as being cooperative, considerate, sharing, thoughtful, and kind.

Here are some ideas about how to promote and teach prosocial skills:

1. Model them yourself. Say "thank you" consistently to children. Every time you are kind, considerate, and sharing with the children, you are modeling prosocial skills.

2. When you set a limit, explain *why*. Let children know the effects of their behavior on others—that hitting hurts, that grabbing toys causes unhappiness.

3. Encourage cooperation. Have activities in which children do things together rather than separately. Instead of always offering individual art projects, try taping butcher paper to a table or wall, make available felt pens or crayons, and let children make a group picture.

4. Find alternative ways to guide and control behavior besides punishment. Punishment may work to curb antisocial behaviors, but it works against teaching prosocial ones, and a side effect of punishment is creating anger that may well be expressed by more antisocial behavior.

5. When there is a conflict, take a problem-solving approach rather than a power stance. Model conflict resolution with other adults and also help children in their dealings with each other. Encourage them to talk to each other rather than to you. Give them the words to use if they need them: "Tell Jessie you don't like it when she takes the toy away from you" and then turn and see what Jessie will say back. Help her make herself understood if she needs help. Help the children see each other's points of view and come to some kind of conclusion. Don't solve their conflict for them. Teach them to solve it themselves.

6. Try to "catch the children being good." Pay attention to a child who shares; one who shows sympathy for another; and one who is being cooperative, considerate, or kind. A simple "I like the way you shared your play dough, Shawn" gives the child both recognition and guidance. I know I've recommended catching children and complimenting them when they are being good many times already in this one small book, but really, considering how important the concept is, I can't say it too often!

Prosocial behavior doesn't just happen when you set limits. You have to promote it—even *teach* it.

26
Teaching Self-Help Skills

The time to emphasize teaching self-help skills is in toddlerhood. The toddler who learned to use a spoon becomes the three-year-old who can use a fork, and eventually the four-year-old who can spread butter with a knife—and the five-year-old who can cut up her own hamburger patty.

It's not always easy to teach toddlers self-help skills. Their strong push toward independence makes them both motivated and resistant. Sometimes they want to do what you want them to do. You won't need to encourage most toddlers to feed themselves or to take off their own shoes and socks. They're anxious to do those sorts of tasks for themselves.

The resistance arises when toddlers' sense of independence conflicts with what you want them to do. You want them to put clothes on, and they want to take clothes off. You want them to climb onto their cots, and they want to play outside. How do you handle them when they resist you?

There is no simple solution for responding to toddlers' resistance, or to the resistance of a young child of *any* age, for that matter. My best advice is to avoid power struggles whenever possible. Whenever you can, make a game out of getting dressed or picking up toys, for example. The more

you can approach a situation in a pleasant, calm, matter-of-fact way, the better. If you can make them think that this is not a big deal, you have at least a possibility of success; but if you come on strong and children perceive that you have a giant stake in the outcome, you'll probably have a fight on your hands. As soon as children—especially toddlers—recognize that they're in a win-or-lose situation, they increase resistance.

Children of any age are more likely to be cooperative if the event following what you want them to do is desirable. Use this situation whenever possible. For example, point out "As soon as you get your shoes on we'll go outside." You can't always arrange things this way, but sometimes you can.

Another way to get their cooperation is to make consequences for delays. For example, you may motivate the children by saying "If you take your shoes off right now and lie down, we'll have time for two stories instead of just one." It is, of course, important to follow through and cut back on the second story if they don't do as expected.

A general rule in teaching self-help skills is *Don't do something for a child that he can do for himself.* Family day care providers responsible for a group of children are more likely to follow this rule (out of pure necessity) than parents with just one child. This is a rule, however, that requires periodic exceptions. All children need extra nurturing now and then. When that is the case it doesn't hurt to do something for a child that he or she is capable of. You can state it in honest terms: "I know you can put on your own shoes, but I see how very much you want me to help you, so this time I'm going to help."

Helping five-, four-, three-, two-, and one-year-olds take responsibility requires a good deal of patience. Often it's faster to do things for them even when you have a group to take care of. It's hard to stand by, hands at your sides, while they fumble with shoes and struggle into their own jackets, but your patience pays off when the confidence and skills they gain make your job easier and easier.

27
Nurturing Curiosity in Children

My husband was the kind of child who took apart everything he could get his hands on—toys, watches, bikes, and roller skates—to "see how they worked." He wanted to know *how* and *why* and *what*. Today he still has a strong desire *to know, to understand,* and *to figure things out*. He has something in common with the inventors and scientists who have contributed so much to modern life. That something is *curiosity*. Curiosity is a valuable trait that serves the individual and the society well.

How can you foster an inquiring attitude without sacrificing your home and yourself? How can you cope with curiosity without curbing it? Here are some suggestions:

1. Provide plenty of hands-on experiences. Give the children materials to explore and experiment with. If you give them tools and an old radio to dismantle, they may not feel the need to work on your family room television set. If you give them goop (cornstarch and water—sometimes called *ooblick*), they may stop squishing the soap in your bathroom. A box of food coloring and some cups of water promote investigation. Cooking is infinitely interesting.

2. Change aspects of the surroundings regularly. When the environment always remains the same, curiosity dwindles. Sometimes just moving furniture helps. Try putting the blocks next to the dollhouse for a change, or introducing dinosaurs into the water-play tub. Rotate toys to increase their value in stimulating curiosity and play.

3. Provide surprises. Children are most curious when things don't work the way children expect. Let them try out magnets on a variety of materials and see if they can predict what will stick. Let them try "float and sink" with some objects that do the unexpected. Introduce a pumice rock into a collection of heavier rocks.

4. Be a resource. Take time out, when you can, to answer questions. Provide hints or tools to help them solve problems. Make available materials that would be needed to carry an idea further.

5. Ask "why" yourself. Model the spirit of inquiry. Lead the children into further explorations with such statements as "I wonder what would happen if ..." or "What makes it do that?" Then stand back and let the children find out for themselves.

6. Protect the children and the environment. Use physical limits as much as possible. Put up barricades rather than making rules. Fence off untouchable flowers. Close doors to forbidden rooms. Curiosity flourishes in a safe environment that doesn't require a lot of "no's."

Curious children grow up to be the curious adults who seek to solve the many mysteries of the universe. You can contribute to the further understanding of humankind by the way you nurture curiosity in the children in your care.

28
Risk Taking

Risk taking relates to age. What is a risk for the younger child is nothing to the older one. The crawler finds the step down into the family room a formidable challenge, while the toddler climbs carefully up and down the four back porch steps; the three-year-old hesitantly climbs the ladder to the low slide in the backyard; the four-year-old pauses before climbing the high ladder to the spiral slide at the park; and the five-year-old climbs the highest ladder on the climbing structure and then holds his breath and slides down the fire pole in the middle of it. Each of these children is taking risks at her own level of development.

Risks are a theme in growth. We seem to be programmed to take risks. Consider, for example, the strong need to get upright that consumes children at around one year of age. It is much safer to stay flat on the floor, yet watch a tot struggle to her feet, risking a fall and even a nasty bump. Feet are very small platforms—not at all secure; but the beginner struggles to a standing position over and over, regardless of the risks

involved. And, of course, that first step is a matter of falling forward and catching one's balance (as is every step afterward). Learning to walk is symbolic of growth; it involves letting go of something, moving out from the stable and secure to the unknown and risky.

Once children start walking, the opportunity to encounter a variety of risks increases. The extent to which each child is willing to take these risks relates to a number of factors, including attachment and a sense of basic trust. The trusting child, one whose needs are well met, is more willing to take risks than the child who puts his or her energy into dealing with distrust, a lack of attachment, and unmet needs.

Some children are born to take risks, both physical and emotional. We all know children who climb up on the kitchen counter before they learn to walk, who enter a group without hesitating, who try to explore far beyond any set limits, or who arrive the first morning in day care as if it were an adventure instead of a threat. These children need to be both appreciated and protected.

Other children avoid risks. They play by themselves rather than approach another child. They shy away from strangers. They stay close to a trusted adult rather than exploring freely. These children need gentle encouragement to branch out. Without help, some children spend a lifetime reacting to each new situation as a threat even when there is no obvious risk involved. These children have much to gain from a family day care provider who believes in the benefits of learning to take risks and helps encourage risk taking.

Adults who shrink and squeal at each little risk the child takes can produce a child who also shrinks and squeals. "Watch out!" "You're going to fall!" "Be careful" echoes the adult repeatedly. "I can't, I CAN'T DO IT!" becomes the theme song of the child.

Children need lots of experience with risk taking when young and protected so that they can experiment with little risks—ones that have sufferable outcomes. If they learn to climb small trees, they will eventually be able to take on bigger ones. The child who is overprotected at the beginning may find her first chance to take risks away from the watchful eyes of parents or caregivers during adolescence, when experiments with risk taking may have severe consequences. Drugs, sex, or driving experiments are far riskier than climbing trees.

It is not easy to allow young children to take risks, especially when they aren't your own children. Child care providers, however, are in the business of education. Education involves challenge, and with challenge comes risk.

For Further Reading

Greenberg, P. (1991). *Character development: Encouraging self-esteem & self-discipline in infants, toddlers, & two-year-olds.* Washington, DC: NAEYC.

National Association for the Education of Young Children. (1989). *Developmentally appropriate practice in early childhood programs serving infants* [Brochure]. Washington, DC: NAEYC.

National Association for the Education of Young Children. (1989). *Developmentally appropriate practice in early childhood programs serving toddlers* [Brochure]. Washington, DC: NAEYC.

National Association for the Education of Young Children. (1990). *Good teaching practices for 4- and 5-year olds* [Brochure]. Washington, DC: NAEYC.

V
Caregiving Routines

29
Infant Caregiving Routines

Caregiving routines, such as feeding, diapering, dressing, and washing, are the times when infants receive a relatively long period of one-to-one interaction with the provider. If the provider finds ways to really focus on each child as an individual during these routine tasks, the children require far less adult attention during the other periods of their day.

When an infant is treated as a member of a team during the routine times, rather than a bottom to be cleaned or a mouth to be fed, benefits accrue. Relationships grow—relationships that help a child come to learn about himself and the world. Infants who are involved in their own care as team members come to anticipate what will happen to them, realize that the world has some predictability, and see the values of cooperation. They learn that they have some power to influence the world and the people in it. They begin to make sense out of life.

Here are some guidelines about using routine times effectively:

Carry out routines in a gentle, consistent, timely manner so that young infants learn to trust that their needs will be met. Don't antici-pate every need before the infant expresses it or always respond at the first whimper; but once the communication has been made and it is clear what the need is, a quick response is called for.

Encourage cooperation and participation. Involve babies in their own care. Ask for a leg or a lift of the bottom. Show what you are doing, and verbalize all the while so that the two of you are focused on the operation itself, not on something else.

Appreciate the older infant's push for independence as she resists your efforts, pushes away the washcloth, or tries to climb off the diapering counter. Continue to try for cooperation even though it may be difficult. Distraction techniques may work, but they give the message that the routine is in your interest, not in the child's. For example, once diapering and feeding become your tasks, not joint ones, the resistance becomes even greater.

It may not seem that changing diapers or giving bottles could possibly be so important. Those kinds of tasks seem to be something you just do automatically without a lot of thought or attention. Most of us have the ability to change a child's clothes, for instance, while on automatic pilot—at the same time putting out fires in one corner of the room, praising the child who is picking up toys in another corner, and even taking time out to answer the telephone. Yet that automatic pilot approach gives a message to the child: "this adult doesn't enjoy dealing with me in this way. I'm not important." Of course, you can

Being treated as a full human being during caregiving routines provides opportunities for babies to satisfy their needs for attention, holding and touching, interaction, and attachment, as well as augmenting cognitive and language skills, all of which contribute to growing self-esteem. All those benefits come from changing diapers time and time again, from providing the hundreds of bottles one baby consumes, from changing clothes and from washing little hands and faces. The time spent in these tasks mounts up. Use it well!

30
Preschool Caregiving Routines

Although caregiving routines don't take as much time for three-, four-, five-, and six-year-old children as they do for infants and toddlers, routines of physical care are still an important part of any young child's day. You don't have a choice about whether or not to meet the physical needs of the children in your care: you have to feed them and provide for their rest and toileting needs; but you do have a choice about the attitude with which you approach these routines. You can look at them as a burden, or you can look at them as important

make up for that message during the other times of the day when you play with and enjoy the child. But why take the chance that the child will take it personally and decide it has to do with his worth as a person? Besides, why waste all those numerous periods together when you could be focusing directly on that one child?

I don't know if you have ever had the experience in the doctor's or dentist's office where you knew that the person working on you was aware and sensitive to the fact that you are a real human being with feelings, needs, and idiosyncrasies. It is quite different from being treated as a tooth to fill or a medical problem to solve.

times for learning, sharing, and building trust through relationships.

Some providers feel resentful about the amount of time and energy taken up by the children's physical needs. If they see themselves as primarily educators, they may regard these routines as outside the curriculum they have in mind for their children. Many people who use *school* as a model for their child care programs would rather eliminate than celebrate the routines related to physical care.

A remark made at a conference on training early childhood educators illustrates this attitude. A college instructor complained when her students' field placement at the campus child care training site came anytime after 11:30 A.M. "My students don't learn anything in the afternoon because all they experience is lunch and naptime," she said.

If those students don't learn anything during the caregiving times, it's because those routines are not regarded as important. There is a good deal to learn during lunch and naptime, both for student teachers and for the children they care for.

What do adults learn? They learn to recognize and meet individual needs in sensitive, nurturing ways. They come to know how to handle groups of children during times when children's feeling thresholds are lowered and the children are less likely to be patient, tolerant, or brave. They learn how to help children feel secure through consistent care. While they are learning all these skills, they also can learn how to take advantage of the "teachable moment."

Children don't necessarily learn what you want them to when you want them to. Many of the most important learnings in a child's life come at odd moments when we least expect them. Routine times often present these moments as adult and child are relating one-to-one about something that is personally meaningful to the child.

Meeting physical needs through caregiving routines is important in early childhood education, no matter what the level and no matter what the setting. Providers who recognize this fact spend less time feeling frustrated and more time promoting development in the children they care for.

31
Two Views of Naptime

Do you have difficulty getting children to sleep after lunch? Perhaps you are ambivalent about whether or not children can or should be required to go to sleep. When adults are not clear, children often respond by resisting.

Some adults are very clear. Here is an example. Molly says that young children need naps, although they don't always recognize the need. Furthermore, she says that **she** needs naptime— her only free time during the long child care day.

"At first it took some effort to train the children to all lie down at the same time. It wasn't easy when I started; but then I discovered such techniques as visually blocking for the children who were distracted by other children by using furniture or other screening devices. There is no question about whether or not children will sleep in my home—they all do."

Jane says, "I hated naps as a child, and it's very hard for me to require that all the children in my care take naps. I much prefer that they discover their own rhythms and rest periodically throughout the day when they need it. Of course, some of the younger children need to be put down—and sometimes they resist, but *I know they need it,* so that isn't hard. Quiet time is all I require for those who don't really need to sleep."

Neither Molly nor Jane have problems with naptime because they are clear about what they believe. Adults who have ambivalent feelings or guilt feelings show hesitations and inconsistencies. They are the ones who have difficulties managing rest time or naptime.

If you have problems with naptime, here are some hints to make it easier:

1. Clarify your feelings and philosophy; then find a way to meet *your* needs *and* the children's.

2. Be sure the children get plenty of fresh air and exercise. Being tired is the best motive for resting.

3. Don't let children get *over*tired. Some children have a hard time settling down when exhausted.

4. Prepare the environment so that the message is "Rest now." An interesting, stimulating play environment calls out to the children. Find another place to rest besides the play room, or turn the play room into a rest room by hiding toys, toning down light, and reducing noise.

5. Create a ritual—a routine—a transition period that gives the message that rest period is coming. If the same thing happens in the same order every day, the children get used to the consistency and come to expect it. Special quiet time stories or music may be part of this ritual.

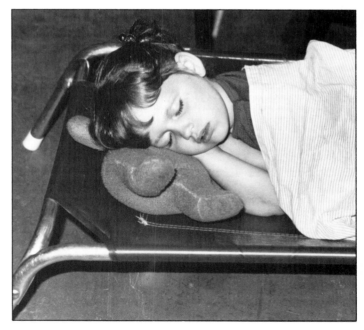

32
Preventing Eating Problems

As always, the best way to approach problems is to prevent them. Theoretically, if you serve a variety of nutritious foods in an attractive way, give some limited choices, and let the children serve themselves, they will eat according to their individual needs; but we all know it doesn't work quite like that.

Some children are picky eaters; others would rather play than eat. What can you do to get children to eat what they need?

1. Don't push. If children feel that you have a great stake in how much they eat and what they eat, they are more likely to "fight back" than go along with your desires. It is easy to get into power struggles over food. Avoid this!

2. Offer limited choices of tasty, nourishing food. Don't give a choice of donuts or oatmeal; the competition is unfair. Too many children will choose fat and sweet over "natural" anytime. Do give choices of apple slices or orange wedges, carrots or celery, cucumbers or tomatoes, and rye bread or whole wheat.

3. Let children serve themselves. You teach them to make decisions about how much they can eat when you let them choose how much to put on their plates. Once they learn how to do this, you can hold them to their decision, which will cut down on food waste.

4. When children are too young to serve themselves (younger than three), serve them a *small* portion of each food to begin with. This way you can give them seconds, rather than urging them to finish their "firsts." Psychologically, this puts you both in a better position and is less likely to invite power struggles.

5. Make meal and snack times pleasant social occasions. Instead of lining up toddlers in highchairs, teach them to sit at low tables in chairs they can get in and out of. Older children can eat together at the kitchen table. If the group is large, it can be divided so that conversation is possible. Seating children in pairs is an alternative to a large, noisy group in which some children dominate others.

6. Don't forget the role that fresh air and exercise play in producing good appetites. Children who are cooped up indoors all day and expected to do quiet activities are less likely to have hearty appetites than those who are free to spend great chunks of time running, jumping, and climbing outdoors in the open air.

As in naptime, there is more than one philosophy about what is important. For example, some caregivers believe it is very important that children make their own choices about how much to eat even if food is wasted. Other caregivers feel strongly about not wasting food and figure out ways to keep that from happening. Children learn what is important to providers when the providers give a clear message.

33
Toilet Training

In all aspects of child care, it is important to understand what the parent wants for his or her child (See the section on parents). Toilet training is no exception. In fact, the first step in toilet training children in your care is to find out the parents' ideas and philosophy on the subject. Not that toilet training can't be done without cooperation at home, but things are bound to be smoother if you and the parents are in agreement about when to start and how to go about it.

Toilet training comes naturally from a cooperative relationship when the child is ready. If you have tried to promote a spirit of cooperation through diapering, when the readiness signs appear you can ease into toilet training with little difficulty.

How do you recognize the signs that a child is ready? Readiness needs to occur in three areas: physical, intellectual, and emotional. The first sign of physical readiness comes about when diapers stay dry for fairly long periods. The child may also tell you when he is wetting or moving his bowels, or perhaps right afterward. Gradually,

from this beginning awareness, the child will learn to control bowel and bladder functions.

Intellectual readiness shows when the child begins to understand where the elimination should take place. Emotional readiness shows when the child is *willing* to perform the way you want.

Avoid power struggles during toilet training; you can't win them. If you have an emotional stake in toilet training, all signs of readiness may disappear. The child may use his increasing ability to control bowel and bladder functions to work against you by holding on when on the potty and letting go once he or she gets up.

Here are some tips about how to facilitate toilet training once you've determined a child is truly ready:

1. Help the child feel physically secure as well as independent. Use a sturdy potty that sits on the floor and doesn't tip. Many children fear sitting up high on the big toilet, and if strapped in for safety, they lose their sense of independence.

2. Ask parents to dress their children in loose, simple clothing that the children can remove themselves. Elastic waistbands work better than overalls, for example.

3. Be patient and relaxed. The less you push, the more likely you are to gain cooperation.

4. Be gentle. Harshness connected with toilet training has harmful, long-term effects.

5. Don't use competition or comparison as a motivator. Competititon in young children is not good for self-esteem or relationships.

Readiness is one key to easy toilet training. Cooperation is another. The more you can get the parents to cooperate, and the more you can get the child to cooperate, the easier your job will be!

34
Cleaning Up

How do you get children to pick up toys and clean up after themselves? Each provider has a bag of tricks. Here are some of mine:

1. Keep your expectations for clean-up appropriate to the age of the child. Expect less of a toddler than a four-year-old. The toddler can be expected to put some of the snap-together plastic blocks into the box where they belong, but she may have an enormous urge to dump them back out again; only your vigilance will prevent this occurrence. The four-year-old can be expected to put all the blocks in the box, put the box back on the shelf where it belongs, and then go over and help put the puzzles away.

2. Keep the environment orderly. If everything has a place, picking up isn't so hard. Children develop a sense of order when they live in an organized environment.

3. Make a game out of picking up toys. Putting things back in their place can give the same joy as working a puzzle. Some children don't even know that it is a dreaded chore. Keep that fact a secret if at all possible by having a positive attitude yourself.

4. Pick up after yourself. Modeling is a good teacher. You don't even have to talk. They get the lesson just by being around you.

Of course it isn't always so easy. Some children arrive in your care with a bad attitude about picking up. They don't see it as fun and games. They don't want to do it.

In this case you have to take a problem-solving approach. Discuss, negotiate, and determine consequences. As a group, you and the children can figure out how to solve this problem if you put your heads together *and* if you are dedicated to the idea that order in the play environment is the responsibility of those who use it.

Don't get into power struggles. Don't make clean-up such a negative experience that kids go to any lengths to avoid it. I know that's easier said than done. I know because I can be a real grouch when faced with both a mess and reluctant children.

Some providers have a need for more order than others. Some continually work to get the children to restore it, while others are willing and able to let the mess accumulate as long as the children are constructively involved in play. In other words, clean-up time may be ongoing, or it may be

sign on very special structures). This becomes a problem if the blocks are then unavailable for other children to work or play with. However, that's the kind of situation that can be problem-solved with a little "sports announcing." You need to help one child know what the other is feeling and help them work out a solution together.

What doesn't work is to let the mess accumulate all day and face it by yourself after all the children are gone. That's not fair to you, and it doesn't teach the children responsibility.

For Further Reading

Greenberg, P. (1991). *Character development: Encouraging self-esteem & self-discipline in infants, toddlers, & two-year-olds.* Washington, DC: NAEYC.

National Association for the Education of Young Children (Producer). (1986). *Caring for infants and toddlers* [Film], with Bettye M. Caldwell. Washington, DC: NAEYC.

National Association for the Education of Young Children. (1990). *Keeping healthy: Parents, teachers, and children* [Brochure]. Washington, DC: NAEYC.

National Association for the Education of Young Children (Producer). (1986). *Seeing infants with new eyes* [Film], with Magda Gerber's program. Washington, DC: NAEYC.

San Fernando Valley Child Care Consortium; A. Godwin & L. Schrag, Co-Chairs. (1996). *Setting up for infant/toddler care: Guidelines for centers and family child care homes.* Rev. ed. Washington, DC: NAEYC.

a scheduled event—say, before lunch. Neither is the "right" way; both work for some providers.

Some providers see a need for children to be involved in ongoing projects and are willing to suspend pickup time in some specific areas. For instance, a block structure may be saved to work on later (one provider even puts a "Please Save"

35
Providing for Free Play

The most important part of your job after keeping children safe and cared for by meeting their physical and emotional needs is providing plenty of time and appropriate space for them to play. Play is a need, too! Play is a most valuable use of a child's time. They learn social skills, develop intellectually, feel powerful, expand their imaginations, refine movement skills, learn and practice language, follow their individual interests, and much, much more. Play is beneficial to children of all ages.

Here's how you can facilitate free play in your home and yard:

1. Set up an environment that invites play. Children need both large spaces to move around in and very small spaces in which to be alone and private. They need things to do that allow them to manipulate objects, to exercise large muscles, to use their imagination, to experience their senses, and to construct and create.

2. Give choices. Free play is facilitated when children can choose from a variety of materials, toys, equipment, and activities. Of course, this may take some creativity on your part, because your resources aren't unlimited. With dedication to the idea of choice, you can find ways to ensure that children can make choices about what and how they want to play.

3. Consider developmental appropriateness. Although your home and yard may remain basically the same no matter what the children's age range, you'll have to take into consideration how to set up when you have babies, toddlers, and preschoolers at the same time, or how to modify when your group is composed mostly of after-school children.

4. Make a reasonable daily schedule that provides for the chunks of time children need to follow their interests, to get involved, and to become absorbed. Because adults mistakenly believe that children have short attention spans, they often create schedules that break time into many small pieces. In that situation, children are always in transition from one activity or place to another, and they learn not to become absorbed in what they are doing.

5. Consider your role during free-play times. Rather than being an entertainer or a teacher, your role should be a facilitator and a resource person. When the children don't need you, there is no reason to interrupt them. When they need help to get started, to make something work, or to get along with each other, you can step in as a facilitator, offering just a small bit of help to get them started or keep them going. When they need something to add to their play, you can consider providing it. (The play has turned to fire engines; are you willing to add a hose? Sarah wants to build a tent; do you have an old bedspread you're willing to bring out?)

Making play rich and full can be one of the most rewarding experiences in family day care. Those times when the children are happily playing are satisfying! They make it all worthwhile.

36
Setting Up the Environment for Play

How you set up the environment can influence the quality of play as well as how hard or easy life is for you as a family day care provider. An environment that is safe, challenging, and invites exploration not only encourages play, which facilitates learning, but eliminates many discipline problems.

Safety is always a first consideration if children are going to explore freely. The next consideration is developmental appropriateness. What is in the environment that encourages each child in your care to experience sensory exploration and problem solving through play? What provides for physical development of both the large muscles of the arms, legs, and trunk, and the small muscles of the fingers, hands, and feet? Do you have objects, toys, furniture, or equipment that allow for each age group to express creativity?

Don't just consider your indoor play space; outdoors is equally important. The same considerations apply.

Providers do not need to turn over all space in their homes to the children in their care. Defining adult spaces as separate from child spaces works quite well and allows adults to continue to enjoy their own homes. The easiest way to separate the child spaces from the adult ones is to close doors or put up barriers.

Children also need personal spaces. Adults help define this space for them by providing individual storage for personal possessions and a sleeping area. Hideaways and nooks are shared personal space that provide much-needed privacy for playing alone during what can be a long, social day care day. If these nooks and crannies are soft, they provide an extra bonus for children.

Behavior is greatly influenced by environment. Environments for children must provide some choice of things to do, but not too many. Both barren environments and overstimulating ones cause behaviors that no one likes. Imagine a group of children in a room or yard with very little in it that they can play with. They are bound to fight over whatever objects are available. They will be busy thinking up mischief if they don't have something available to use up the energy children are so famous for.

Conversely, an environment with too much to choose from also causes problems. The grocery store is an illustration of this kind of environment

51

because the built-in allure encourages children to touch and take. Home play spaces can provide the same problem if everything you have is out on display calling, "touch me, take me!"

Keep home play spaces manageable by putting away toys or objects if you have an overabundance. The right number of things around to play with makes life easier; too many creates chaos, as does too few.

Open-ended materials such as sand or water give children a chance to experience a sense of power as they create, manipulate, feel, and explore the properties of the material. Open-ended materials can also be soothing, as can soft materials.

By providing appropriate play space, objects, encouragement, and physical limits, you help the children in your care to see themselves as "doers." This is an important step in their continuing ability to be good learners and fully functioning adults.

=== 37 ===
The Benefits of Outdoor Play

There's no such thing as bad weather, only inadequate clothing. That's what they say in Sweden, where they take their children outside to play during summer and winter—even in subzero temperatures. The children are healthier for it.

Children need fresh air and vigorous exercise every day. They can't get either very well indoors. With a group of people in a room together, all breathing the same air, the room gets stale quickly. Fresh air outside renews vigor, clears the brain, and helps children function better.

Exercise has the same effect because the blood reaches the brain more quickly and clears the system. Children eat better, sleep better, and think better when they get adequate fresh air and exercise.

Children don't get sick from being outside in cold weather; they get healthy. Illness comes from viruses and bacteria, which are spread much more easily when children are inside in close contact with one another.

See for yourself one of these days when it's cold or rainy and you're cooped up inside. Put on whatever you need to keep warm and dry, go outside, and take a walk. I guarantee you'll feel better afterward.

In the summer providers may keep children indoors because of the heat. But two tried-and-true heatbeaters can take care of that problem: shade and water. Trees or covered patios are handy if they already exist. If they don't, umbrellas or cloth stretched on poles will also work. And for water, all you need is a hose. Of course there are infinite variations on the water theme; for example, buckets, tubs, and plastic wading pools. A day at the beach was created by a provider who dug out a portion of her sandbox (with lots of help from the children), put plastic on the bottom, replaced the sand, and put the hose in. Voila! Just putting the hose in the sandbox without the plastic will also satisfy. And don't forget water painting. Big brushes, buckets of water, and a little concrete will satisfy children for hours and hours on hot days.

Be sure not to regard your outdoor time as a "recess" from learning. Learning can take place anywhere, and some valuable lessons occur more easily outdoors than inside. Of course, there are some toys and materials you want to protect by keeping them inside, but most things can easily be used outside. Books can be carried out to the grass under the trees in the back yard for an impromptu, or even planned, story time. Science, both planned and unplanned, can be carried on outside. In fact, most things that can be learned inside can also be learned outside.

Expanding your learning environment to the outdoors provides many benefits, not the least of which are exercise, fresh air, and a sense of freedom.

38
Taming the Troops: Ideas for Calming Groups of Children

Play time can get wild and unruly at times, and providers need ways to bring calm back into the room or yard. Some ways I know to restore tranquility are:

1. Deliberately slow down your pace. If you are frantic, nervous, and racing around, the children will be too. If you are calm, you may influence the children just by your quiet presence.
2. Help children create small worlds in which to use play figures, because their own world is necessarily restricted when they have to stay indoors. Trays of sand or salt are one way to do this, with small cars, small dolls, action figures, or creatures of various sorts. Add figures to the building blocks for more small world play.
3. If you can't go outside, you need to find some way, everyday, for all the children to engage in gross motor activities. It is important that they jump, run, tumble, climb, bend, and stretch regularly. If nothing else, do calisthenics at circle time. You can't expect kids to be calm if they haven't had enough exercise.
4. Provide get-away spots. Some children are overstimulated by long hours with large groups of children. If they have places to be alone or with just a few children, they can calm themselves down. A cushioned closet with books to read is a solution in some family day care homes; cardboard boxes, tents, dog houses, and tables with bedspreads over them, all provide small retreats for children who need them. Even pulling a couch out from the wall and letting children hide behind it can work. Find a way to provide nooks and crannies, and encourage children to seek them out when they need less stimulation. (Don't use them to punish!)

5. Take good care of yourself. If you're especially tired, not feeling well, or overburdened with more to do than you have time for, you're bound to be irritated by even normal noisy behavior. Get enough rest, eat right, and get plenty of exercise.

I have already discussed ways to keep children from becoming too wild. These are additional suggestions.

39
Using Play Activities To Teach Cooperation

Most of us value cooperation, but few experiences in our own educational backgrounds have taught us how to teach it to young children. In early childhood education, we sometimes spend so much time valuing each child as an individual that we overlook teaching those same individuals to be cooperative.

The mixed-age groups of most family day care homes promote cooperation because older children can help the younger ones. You can encourage group endeavors such as plays, gardening, or even building a play yard structure from planks, boxes, and ladders.

There are some ways of doing ordinary activities that particularly encourage cooperation. Here are some sample ideas:

• Cooperative art projects: Try a wood-scrap gluing project that produces one big sculpture instead of lots of little ones. You might find you end up with something decorative enough to put on display! For younger children, you can begin a cooperative collage by mounting a piece of contact paper, sticky side out, and offering things to stick to it. Older children can work on a quilt together—something to decorate the playroom wall.

• Cooperative music: If you have three xylophones instead of just one, children can experiment with playing together. Rhythm instruments encourage cooperation because children play with each other in time to the music.

• Some equipment that demands cooperation: Large hollow blocks are too big for young children to carry alone. They can solicit help from other children if you encourage them to do so. A teeter-totter takes two to work; so does a stretcher. A less-traditional piece of equipment designed to get kids to cooperate is a one-rope, two-seat swing slung over pulleys; it only works with two children, each counterbalancing the weight of the other.

Of course, it isn't just activities or equipment that counts when teaching cooperation—it's your whole attitude. You can find many simple ways to encourage children to cooperate with each other once you focus on this goal. I think you'll find the results well worth the effort.

═══ 40 ═══
The Benefits of Pretend Play

With or without props, most young children, even toddlers, engage in playing pretend on a regular basis. This type of imaginative play is a valuable use of children's time. Through it they create mental images and learn to deal with the world in a symbolic way. They transform reality and practice mastery over it. They recreate and reconstruct what has happened in the past in order to release pent-up emotions.

Toddlers play in what my son calls the bang-bang baby way. Their play is mostly action with a few sound effects or perhaps words to augment it. The three-year-old begins creating dialogues, many of which are imitations of the adults in her life, to go along with the action, which is also mostly imitation. By the age of five, children create involved stories and act out complex roles. School-age children continue to expand in their ability to imagine and create worlds of their own.

Here are three ways to encourage creative, imaginative, pretend play in your home:

1. Provide experiences that the children can replay. A trip to the store, fire station, or a parent's office gives children material for their play.

2. Provide props. Having dress-up clothes always available invites creative play. Be sure you include both male and female clothing. Office play is encouraged with a few stamps and an ink pad, an old adding machine, some paper, and writing instruments. A wagon, a hose, and a couple of fire hats are almost sure to result in firefighter play.

3. Allow free expression. Children often work through anger symbolically. You may not be happy to see children expressing pretend anger, but they are getting it out of their systems in a healthy way. Let them express their feelings as long as they don't hurt themselves, other children, or objects and materials.

4. Give plenty of uninterrupted time and space for creative play to evolve. Overscheduling can cut down on rich, dramatic play.

Watch how children work through the events in their lives. By dealing with their feelings in an imaginary situation, children can actually change the way they feel about something. The child who replays the airplane trip he is to take is getting a grip on the fears that may be a part of this experience.

Through pretend play, children gain social skills as they try on various roles to see how things feel from someone else's perspective. They learn to negotiate and cooperate when the pretend play involves more than one person. They gain a sense of power. They gain all that—just from playing "house" or "firefighters"!

For Further Reading

Baker, K. R. (1966). *Let's play outdoors*. Washington, DC: NAEYC.

Blakely, B., Blau, R., Brady, E. H., Streibert, C., Zavitkovsky, A., & Zavitkovsky, D. (1984). *Activities for school-age child care*. Washington, DC: NAEYC.

Brown, J. F. (Ed.). (1982). *Curriculum planning for young children.* Washington, DC: NAEYC.

Carlsson-Paige, N., & Levin, D. E. (1985). *Helping young children understand peace, war, and the nuclear threat.* Washington, DC: NAEYC.

Engstrom, G. (Ed.). (1971). *The significance of the young child's motor development.* Washington, DC: NAEYC.

Greenberg, P. (1991). *Character development: Encouraging self-esteem & self-discipline in infants, toddlers, & two-year-olds.* (pp. 67-74, 101-150, 161-166). Washington, DC: NAEYC.

Hill, D. M. (1977). *Mud, sand, and water.* Washington, DC: NAEYC.

Jalongo, M. R. (1988). *Young children and picture books: Literature from infancy to six.* Washington, DC: NAEYC.

Kamii, C., & DeVries, R. (1980). *Group games in early education: Implications of Piaget's theory.* Washington, DC: NAEYC.

Kritchevsky, S. & Prescott, E., with Walling, L. (1977). *Planning environments for young children: Physical space.* Washington, DC: NAEYC.

Lasky, L. & Mukerji, R. (1980). *Art: Basic for young children.* Washington, DC: NAEYC.

McCracken, J. B. (1987). *More than 1, 2, 3: The real basics of mathematics* [Brochure]. Washington, DC: NAEYC.

McCracken, J. B. (1987). *Play is FUNdamental* [Brochure]. Washington, DC: NAEYC.

McDonald, D. T. (1979). *Music in our lives.* Washington, DC: NAEYC.

National Association for the Education of Young Children. (1990). *El juego es FUNdamental* [Brochure]. Washington, DC: NAEYC.

National Association for the Education of Young Children (Producer). (1986). *Environments for young children* [Film], with Elizabeth Prescott and Elizabeth Jones. Washington, DC: NAEYC.

National Association for the Education of Young Children. (1991). *Facility design for early childhood programs resource guide (revised edition).* Washington, DC: NAEYC.

National Association for the Education of Young Children (Producer). (1990). *Music across the curriculum* [Film], with Thomas Moore. Washington, DC: NAEYC.

National Association for the Education of Young Children. (1990). *Playgrounds: Safe and sound* [Brochure]. Washington, DC: NAEYC.

National Association for the Education of Young Children. (1985). *Toys: Tools for learning* [Brochure]. Washington, DC: NAEYC.

Sawyers, J. K., & Rogers, C. S. (1988). *Helping young children develop through play: A practical guide for parents, caregivers, and teachers,* Washington, DC: NAEYC.

Schickedanz, J. A. (1983). *Helping children learn about reading* [Brochure]. Washington, DC: NAEYC.

Seefeldt, C., & Warman, B. (1990). *Young and old together.* Washington, DC: NAEYC.

Skeen, P., Garner, A. P., & Cartwright, S. (1984). *Woodworking with young children.* Washington, DC: NAEYC.

Stone, J. G. (1990). *Teaching preschoolers: It looks like this . . . in pictures.* Washington, DC: NAEYC.

Sullivan, M. (1982). *Feeling strong, feeling free: Movement exploration for young children.* Washington, DC: NAEYC.

Vergeront, J. (1987). *Places and spaces for preschool and primary (indoors).* Washington, DC: NAEYC.

Vergeront, J. (1988). *Places and spaces for preschool and primary (outdoors).* Washington, DC: NAEYC.

41

The Importance of Parents

Although parents have not played a big role in this little book, in reality they play a very big part in your child care program. Although they are not present during the day, they are behind-the-scenes players in the drama of your day-to-day life with the children in your care.

Parents are where the children come from to you and where they will go when they are no longer in your care; both on a daily basis and on a long-term basis. Parents are the children's primary attachment (usually), and although some of their children may become very attached to you, this attachment is not of the duration of parent attachment. You have no control over how long they will remain in your home—no control over when it will be time to say good-bye—and for almost all children and their providers that day eventually comes.

It is up to you to provide for good short-term attachment, but not get so involved that your heart is broken when the family moves away or the child leaves your care for some other reason. This advice isn't only for your own good—but also for the child's sake. Leaving a provider can be as painful as losing a parent if the attachment has been allowed to grow too strong and seemingly permanent.

You are not the parent; you are a supplement to the parent—a daily temporary substitute. With this in mind, you will try to downplay any competition for a child's affection that may arise between you and the parent. It's not easy to avoid competition with parents, whether the feelings come from you or from them, but when you are aware of the dangers—the conflicts that the situation creates in all of you, including the child—you will do what you can to get out of a competitive mode and into a cooperative one.

Another feeling you may have about parents is resentment. Sometimes providers believe the parents have the "better deal" because they arrive in the morning dressed to the teeth, ready to sit in a quiet office somewhere; take long lunch hours; or move off into a challenging, interesting business, intellectual, or social world, leaving you to deal with the fussing, the runny noses, and the mess involved in the care and education of their children.

Or perhaps parents resent you. After all you get to stay home, in your own territory; you get to be your own boss, while they have to face the cold, cruel world, separated from the children they love—the children you get to enjoy and experience all day.

In spite of all these feelings, parents and providers must form a partnership. They must see themselves as a team working for the good of the child. This isn't easy, but it's vital.

42
Parent-Provider Relations

The most important part of the family day care providers' job is to establish a good relationship with the parents of the children they care for. Keep in mind that the parent is your client, not the child, although sometimes it is tempting to put your focus on the child and forget the parent.

From my experience, I have discerned three stages of development of people who work in child care—both in family day care and in centers. Not all providers go through these stages, but some do. The first stage early childhood educators have long called the *savior* stage. Savior providers find themselves with a strong feeling that makes them wish they could rescue children from their parents.

During the second stage, which I call the *parents-as-clients* stage, the providers' feeling may be the same, but the approach is different. Instead of wanting to rescue the children themselves, they want to educate the parents so the children won't need saving. Providers in this stage see their job, indeed the hope for the children, as parent education. A shift occurs as the parent becomes the client instead of the child. Of course, it's fine to educate parents—I'm all for parent education; but if the savior glow is still on the provider, the education is bound to be less than effective. I

know when I've been in a situation in which someone was trying to "educate" me about my children from a superior position, I've done some strong resisting.

The ultimate stage comes when the providers see themselves as partners with parents. It is from this third *parents-as-partners* stage that clear communication arises as the parent and provider *share* in the care of the child. Providers in this stage are aware of the importance of the strength of the parent-child attachment. Although the child may fit in very well with the provider's family, providers are careful to do nothing that weakens the child's sense of belonging to his own family.

When providers and parents are partners, the communication is two-way, as is the education.

Providers share what they know about child development and about the child in the day care setting. Parents share what they know of their own children, including some history.

Parents also share their goals and desires for their children, as well as specifics, such as their children's habits, special needs, ways of communicating, and daily routine. For the very young child this includes such information as when and how much sleep can be expected, how the child goes to sleep, eating preferences and habits, bowel function, comfort strategies, and so on.

Communication about specifics should occur when the child first enters the home and continue on an ongoing basis thereafter. The ongoing communication can occur during those drop-off and pick-up times and at scheduled conferences.

How much you want to do beyond exchanging actual child care information is up to you. Some providers find themselves in the position of actually parenting the parents because they are sought out to provide support. You have to decide for yourself how much of this service you want to perform. You have some choices: You can provide what the parent needs, keeping in mind the goal of helping that parent to eventually become self-sufficient; you can redirect the parent to someone else such as a counselor; or you can get the parents together with one another and encourage them to form a mutual support system.

The parent-provider relationship is so important that it is worth putting some energy into focusing on it. Clarify how you feel about parents, individually and as a group. Find out how they feel about you. How can you and the parents work together to develop a healthy, mutually beneficial relationship?

43

Some Specifics About Communicating With Parents

As has just been said, a key to your success as a family day care provider is your ability to communicate with parents. Here are some tips about how to do that:

1. Make yourself available to parents when possible. Quick exchanges at arrival and departure times can be profitable communication periods, even though the environment may be hectic. At least these periods occur daily, and they add up if well used, even for just a couple of minutes a day. Sometimes it's difficult to take yourself away from the children for more than a fast word or two, but if you let the parent know that you are willing to talk at a more convenient time, sometimes that can be arranged.

2. Make parents feel comfortable about exchanging information with you. Be open and available, and be aware that environment also affects communication. If you keep parents standing outside your front door while you're keeping your ear on the kids roaring around the living room, you convey a different message than if you have the children involved in activities and then invite the parents in to sit down (assuming he or she has time). Of course, you must protect yourself from parents feeling *too* welcome and taking advantage of you. After all you have both a job and a life of your own, so you may need to change the situation if parents just come in and sit down like your best friend or part of your family.

3. Unless you have a good memory, keep records so you can report specifics about a child to her parents. This is especially important if you care for infants. Parents need to know when and how much their babies ate, when they slept and how long, as well as information about bowel and bladder function.

4. Report anecdotes. Some providers actually write down the interesting little events that occur during the day and send them home or verbally report them in detail to the parents. Other providers depend on their memories. Parents appreciate these little stories of the incidents they miss. Be careful, however, of making the parent feel bad about missing out on a first. If you're the one who sees the first step, you might consider not passing it on so the parent can tell you the next day that his baby took that first step at home.

5. Develop your listening skills. Often behind a stream of parent words lies quite a different message from what the words seem to express. Try to understand what the message is. If a feeling is being expressed, pick up on it and feed it back to the parent; you'll open up communication channels. ("You sound really upset!") It's the same kind of thing you do with children; it's effective with adults as well.

6. Regard communication as a two-way process. If you're having trouble with a child, invite the parents' input. What might be happening at home that would contribute to this behavior? What might the daycare experience be contributing to a problem? Is the parent worried about it? How can the two of you together figure out what to do?

A theme of this book has been *problem solving*. Though most communication between parent and provider has little to do with problems, as a provider you have many opportunities to develop and practice problem-solving—conflict-management— skills with parents. Taking a problem-solving attitude will help you look at problems as challenges that you and the parents face together, and you can take a positive approach to solving them. Learn to clarify what the real issues are. Learn to become a good negotiator. These skills are part of effective communication.

44
Multicultural Issues

Communication is not easy, especially between adults who care for the same child. Even when these two—parent and provider—are of the same culture, difficulties arise. Even more potential difficulties arise when the provider and parent are of different cultures.

Imagine a provider and parent who had very different ideas about toilet training. One sees toilet training as a means of eliminating diapers and is anxious to start as soon as possible by "catching" the baby as young as possible and putting him or her on the potty before the diaper is used. The other sees toilet training as an important step toward developing independence and therefore believes it should start only when children are ready for this responsibility. Because of my culture, I come from the readiness school and therefore wrote the toilet training section from that point of view. That's not the only point of view. Matters of elimination are very cultural, as are other values. The value difference in this example is that the first adult values interdependence, whereas the second adult values independence. Imagine the conflict these two will have if they are sharing the care of a child!

Here's another area of conflict: eating. Imagine a provider and a parent who differed in their views of self-help skills. One is not interested in

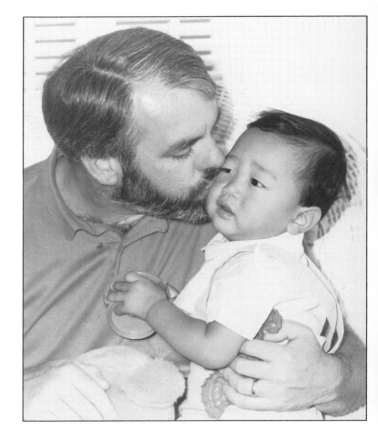

babies learning to take care of their own needs until they are way beyond babyhood. She values a clean, neat, orderly mealtime, which she accomplishes by spoon-feeding children who are not able to eat in a mannerly, orderly fashion. The other adult is shocked by what she calls "keeping the child a baby." She believes that children should feed themselves—experience all the sensory aspects of a mealtime—be in control of how much they eat and how they eat it. She believes that a child who is spoon-fed beyond infancy is being deprived.

Take holding as another example. One adult believes that babies should be held all the time because they need the human body to provide security and comfort. This adult sees the first few years as extensions of the womb and tries to duplicate the prenatal experience as much as possible. Another adult believes that babies need to be held, but not all the time. This adult sees much value in putting babies, even those who can't crawl yet, on the floor, where they can squirm, roll, and wiggle around to their heart's content. These adults see being held as much too confining. They worry that development is being hampered.

These adults are going to have some real conflicts if they find themselves in a relationship with each other in the provider or parent roles. "Right" and "wrong" methods are tied to culture, so there is no way for one to win an argument over the other. The only answer is communication. There must be some value sorting and some give-and-take if the adult pairs in each of these examples are to care for the same child.

Get out your problem-solving skills if you find yourself on the opposite side of a caregiving issue such as those previously mentioned. You'll need to sharpen those skills if you are going to share the care of the child of a parent who disagrees with you. You're also going to need some cultural education if that parent happens to be of a culture different from yours. You can also *give* some cultural education, but it won't be easy!

For further reading

Derman-Sparks, L., Gutiérrez, M., & Phillips, C. (1989). *Teaching young children to resist bias: What parents can do* [Brochure]. Washington, DC: NAEYC.

Dittman, L. L. (1990). *Finding the best care for your infant or toddler* [Brochure]. Washington, DC: NAEYC.

Greenberg, P. (1991). *Character development: Encouraging self-esteem & self-discipline in infants, toddlers, & two-year-olds* (pp. 56–57), Washington, DC: NAEYC.

McCracken, J. B. (1990). *Merrily we roll along* [Brochure]. Washington, DC: NAEYC.

McCracken, J. B. (1990). *Off to a sound start: Your baby's first year* [Brochure]. Washington, DC: NAEYC.

National Association for the Education of Young Children. (1990). *Como escoger un buen programa de educación pre-escolar* [Brochure]. Washington, DC: NAEYC.

National Association for the Education of Young Children. (1990). *How to choose a good early childhood program* [Brochure]. Washington, DC: NAEYC.

National Association for the Education of Young Children. (1990). *Media violence and children: A guide for parents* [Brochure]. Washington, DC: NAEYC.

National Association for the Education of Young Children (Producer). (1989). *Partnerships With Parents* [Film]. Washington, DC: NAEYC.

National Association for the Education of Young Children. (1988). *Testing of young children: Concerns and cautions* [Brochure]. Washington, DC: NAEYC.

National Association for the Education of Young Children. (1991). *What are the benefits of high quality programs?* [Brochure]. Washington, DC: NAEYC.

Conclusion

Family day care is the backbone and mainstay of the child care delivery system of the United States. Family day care providers supply a much-needed service, one without which this country would be paralyzed. Can you imagine if family day care disappeared for one day? Business and industry would stop, machines would grind to a halt, computer screens would be blank, and stores would close. We couldn't function without the service of the family day care providers. They are important!

Not only are they important, they are professionals—in business and education. Most educators don't know business and most business people don't have skills as educators. Experienced family day care providers have skills and knowledge in two fields.

Family day care providers are valuable, but not everyone recognizes this yet. We live in a society that is just waking up to the fact that the future of America depends on the quality of upbringing our children receive. The future generation, those in whose hands the country will lie, are being raised *right now*. That future generation is the one that will take care of you and me in our old age. How that generation turns out depends on how well they are being cared for. The fact is that a great number of the members of the next generation are being raised in day care—both family day care homes and centers.

It is time the whole of society wakes up to the fact that we cannot afford *not* to give our children the very best. The early years are too important! I'm talking about issues of quality—high quality. The problem is that we haven't yet clearly defined what quality is when it comes to family day care. We're getting closer to recognizing quality in center care, but quality in institutions doesn't necessarily translate in a literal manner to family day care. A problem occurs when criteria for quality in centers are applied to a home setting. The message is that centers are better than homes, and I resist that message mightily!

What I would like to do is to give family day care providers permission to move away from an institutional image, back off from the teacher model, and feel free to create a different set of criteria for quality than that used for centers. I have seen numerous examples of approaches in family day care homes that ensure that children's needs are met while opening those children's minds and leading them to examine, explore, and learn about the world in their own unique ways.

My dream is that one day, quality in family day care will be recognized for what it is, although it may be different from quality in centers. I also long for the day when providers will be given the credit they deserve for their contribution to helping raise, care for, and educate the next generation.

Additional Resources

Books

Bredekamp, S., & Copple, C. (Eds.). (1997). *Developmentally appropriate practice in early childhood programs*. Rev. ed. Washington, DC: NAEYC.

Bronson, M.B. (1995). *The right stuff for children birth to 8: Selecting play materials to support development*. Washington, DC: NAEYC.

Diffily, D., & Morrison, K. (Eds.). (1996). *Family friendly communication for early childhood programs*. Washington, DC: NAEYC.

Goffin, S.G., & Lombardi, J. (1988). *Speaking out: Early childhood advocacy*. Washington, DC: NAEYC.

Katz, L.G., Evangelou, D., & Hartman, J.A. (1990). *The case for mixed-age grouping in early childhood education*. Washington, DC: NAEYC.

Kendrick, A.S., Kaufmann, R., & Messenger, K.P. (1995). *Healthy young children: A manual for programs—1995 edition*. Washington, DC: NAEYC.

Kontos, S. (1992). *Family day care: Out of the shadows and into the limelight*. Washington, DC: NAEYC.

Modigliani, K., Reiff, M., & Jones, S. (1987). *Opening your door to children: How to start a family day care program*. Washington, DC: NAEYC.

Rivkin, M.S. (1995). *The great outdoors: Restoring children's right to play outside*. Washington, DC: NAEYC.

Zero to Three, National Center for Infants, Toddlers, and Families. (1995). *Caring for infants and toddlers in groups: Developmentally appropriate practice*. Washington, DC: Author.

Brochures

Beginner's bibliography—1997. Washington, DC: NAEYC.

Careers in early childhood education. Washington, DC: NAEYC.

A caring place for your toddler. Washington, DC: NAEYC.

A good kindergarten for your child. Washington, DC: NAEYC.

A good preschool for your child. Washington, DC: NAEYC.

How to plan and start a good early childhood program. Washington, DC: NAEYC.

Love & learn: Discipline for young children. Washington, DC: NAEYC.

NAEYC position statement on licensing and public regulation of early childhood programs. Washington, DC: NAEYC.

Play is FUNdamental. Washington, DC: NAEYC. Also available in Spanish.

Young children and African-American literature. Washington, DC: National Black Child Development Institute.

Periodicals

The CF Child Care Bulletin. The Children's Foundation, 725 15th Street, N.W., Suite 505, Washington, DC 20005. Newsletter written for providers. Information, current issues, association news, and program ideas.

The Garden. Windflower Enterprises, 142 South Claremont Street, Colorado Springs, CO 80910. Quarterly newsletter for family child care providers and agencies that provide support to them. Reports on issues of interest to the family child care community, especially relating to professionalism and professional development.

Young Children. National Association for the Education of Young Children, 1509 16th Street, N.W., Washington, DC 20036-1426. The bimonthly, professional journal of NAEYC. Keeps members abreast of the latest developments in early childhood education with its readable yet scholarly approach to research and theory and its emphasis on expert classroom practice.

Videos

Before and after school . . . creative experiences. Indiana Steps Ahead Child Care Video Series. Washington, DC: NAEYC.

Designing developmentally appropriate days. Indiana Steps Ahead Child Care Video Series. Washington, DC: NAEYC.

Early intervention: Natural environments for children. Indiana Steps Ahead Child Care Video Series. Washington, DC: NAEYC.

Painting a positive picture: Proactive behavior management. Indiana Steps Ahead Child Care Video Series. Washington, DC: NAEYC.

Quality family child care. Indiana Steps Ahead Child Care Video Series. Washington, DC: NAEYC.